BETTY HENDERSON

GRACE

FOR EVERY TRIAL

journeyforth®

Greenville, South Carolina

Grace for Every Trial: A Women's Bible Study
Betty Henderson

Design by Rita Golden
Page layout by Kelley Moore

© 2008 by BJU Press
Greenville, South Carolina 29614
JourneyForth Books is a division of BJU Press

Printed in the United States of America
All rights reserved

ISBN 978-1-59166-918-0

15 14 13 12 11 10 9 8 7 6 5 4 3

Dedicated to the following families who, while suffering great loss, were examples to all because they responded biblically to sorrow and suffering. Their responses brought glory to God and their friends, who watched and received instruction.

Cliff and Barbara Krause
Dale and Marti Nye
John and Susan Ridley
Steve, Mark, Rebecca, and Matthew Spencer
Tony and Ellen Slutz
Dwight and Carolyn Williams
Jim and Gayle Roschi

Take this book in Thy wounded hand,
Jesus, Lord of Calvary.
Let it go forth at Thy command,
Use it as it pleaseth Thee.

(Missionary and sufferer, Amy Carmichael,
1867–1951)

CONTENTS

Preface vii

LESSON 1   "My Servant Job" 1

LESSON 2   Responding to Sorrow 11

LESSON 3   Job's Visitors 19

LESSON 4   Job's Fainting Fit 30

LESSON 5   Pity for the Pitiful 40

LESSON 6   More Words at the Dump 50

LESSON 7   "Yet Will I Trust Him" 61

LESSON 8   Words: Weary and Wondrous 71

LESSON 9   "I Shall Come Forth as Gold" 82

LESSON 10   "Be Still, Job!" 93

LESSON 11   "How Great Thou Art" 103

LESSON 12   Job's Happy Ending 114

Endnotes 125

PREFACE

While working on this Bible study, more than a few eyebrows have been raised when I mentioned the study is on the book of Job. Your eyebrows may also be a bit arched as you think, "Why on earth do women need to study Job? Isn't that a book relegated only to the halls of higher learning?" My answer to you is that women sitting around tables in fellowship halls can, with much profit, also study this oldest of Bible books.

I realize Job may not be voted the favorite Bible book of the majority of women—or men. Aside from the first two chapters and chapter 42, most of Job is foreign territory to believers. However, the thirty-nine chapters hedged between these are filled with golden truths. Throughout these often unread pages, our God has scattered wonderful truths about Himself and His sovereignty over all creation.

Job is not just a book about the suffering and patience of its main character. I'm afraid this is the untrue conclusion of many believers. Some wrongly think that studying Job may bring the test of suffering to their own lives. While Job and his suffering is a theme in the book, it is not the main theme. As I've studied Job, I have discovered so many other profitable truths. Here are just four we will consider in this study:

- God is sovereign, or in complete charge, over all the events of Job's life—and our own.

- The long-suffering of God, not just the suffering of Job, is a thread beautifully woven throughout Job's pages. The faithfulness and greatness of God, and the weakness and pride of sinful man, are also displayed here for our admonition.

- Job's response to his loss and suffering, as well as the responses of his wife and friends, reminds us of the need to have biblical, not fleshly, responses when God sends sorrow and affliction into our lives.

- A compassionate response to those who are suffering is another important foundational truth found in Job. From Job's friends we can learn how to be merciful, not miserable, comforters.

Yes, the book of Job is ancient, but its truths and insights are amazingly modern. After all, every word was given by our unchanging God, and can any portion of His Word ever be outdated? The message of Job is needed today more than ever. Will you allow the Lord to open your eyes so that you may see wonderful and amazing things from this book? God wrote it as a testimony to His servant Job and as a holy instruction book for His servants of every century.

"MY SERVANT JOB"

"Hast thou considered my servant Job, that there
is none like him in the earth?" (Job 1:8)

SCRIPTURE TO READ: Job 1:1–12

As we open the door of this oldest book in the Bible, we are, initially, treated to a picture of true happiness when we are introduced to Job's large family. As we tour his large estate, we learn that while Job had much wealth in cattle and lands, that was not where his true wealth lay. A wise man who lived centuries after Job stated that "the blessing of the Lord, it maketh rich" (Proverbs 10:22). Job had walked with God for many years, and all his earthly possessions were testimony to the blessing of God on his life.

We need to enjoy the happiness displayed in Job 1. It will soon disappear, and there will be little or no joy again until we reach Job 42. The reason for this unhappiness is found in Job 1:6–12. We read of an unusual meeting between the wicked "prince of this world" (John 12:31) and the King of Kings. God honored Job before Satan by describing him with words used for only a few of His servants. But Satan also had his own words to describe the greatest man on the earth. From this meeting the foundation is set for all that happens in Job.

1. Who wrote the book of Job? Find the answer in a Bible dictionary or a good study Bible.

   We don't know who authored the book

Suggestions from Bible scholars about who wrote the book have included Job, Moses, Solomon, or Elihu, the fourth friend who visited Job on the ash heap.

2. Read 2 Peter 1:21. Who is the heavenly author of Scripture? According to Peter, what kind of men did He use to write the Bible?

   men who were directed by the Holy Spirit

3. Where did Job live (Job 1:1)?

   _Uz_

This ancient land is thought to be in or near the area known as Edom, or Northern Arabia. Today we know much of this area as Saudi Arabia. There is also sometimes a question as to when Job lived. Most Bible scholars believe he could have lived before God gave the law to Moses. Others, however, claim he lived before Abraham. If this is so, we can place Job between the events in Genesis 11–12.

4. Read verse 1 again. God used the following words to describe Job's character and spiritual life. What do you think it means to be

~~Perfect~~ Blameless

a man whose heart sought to please God - who repented of his sin

Upright before God

Kept God in the forfront of his mind - was intentional.

God fearing

a man who understood the magnatude of who/what God is - Alpha/omega

One who eschews (turns from) evil

who lives life with intentionality

It is also interesting to remember early in this study that Job was not an Israelite. He lived in a pagan culture as Abraham did. Like Abraham, he turned his heart to worship the true and living God and made Him the center of his life. "Do we fear God? Do we take seriously the gospel of Jesus Christ in the midst of the pagan culture of our modern world? It is a great challenge, but it can be done. Job is proof of that, and that is why his experience is preserved in the revelation of Scripture."[1]

5. Are these characteristics of Job still requirements for those who would walk with God? What do the following verses command of believers?

Matthew 5:48

To be imitators of God - His Character

Psalm 34:9

fear the Lord

Psalm 34:14–16

Be intentional - Depart from evil - do good - seek peace - Look to the Lord

Psalm 84:11

to walk upright

6. According to Job 1:3, what material blessings had God entrusted to Job?

   7000 sheep, 3000 camels, 500 yoke of oxen (1000), 500 female donkeys, and many servants

7. What was the title given to Job in 1:3? What does this mean?

   Greatest of all men in the East = fame, power, wealth

8. After observing all Job's lands, servants, and cattle, let's look now at his family. Read Job 1:2 and then describe Job's family.

   Seven sons and 3 daughters —

What words in 1:4–5 do you read to suggest he had a happy family? What good times did they enjoy together? It is important to remember that during Job's time, fathers were the religious leaders of their families. There were no priests to instruct fathers in the law of God, which was yet to be given. Therefore, Job dutifully acted as the priest for his family when he offered sacrifices before God for the forgiveness of their sins.

9. Read Job 1:5 again. How did Job specifically show spiritual leadership and concern for his children?

   He prayed for them and lived out an example of godliness.

In just a few words, the Holy Spirit tells us about Job's role as a godly father. What time of day did he bring his children before God? How often did he do this?

> Mark well that he offered according to the number of his children. He did not leave out one. If he prayed for the eldest, he prayed for the youngest too, and if he made

supplication for the sons, he did not forget the daughters, Ah, parents, never forget any of your children, carry them all before God, let them all be consecrated to Him. . . . I say then my friends that Job did this continually, which teaches the parent his duty of continually pleading for his sons and daughters.[2]

From this lovely scene on earth picturing Job and his children, we turn to an unusual meeting between God and our adversary, the Devil. From the first five verses of Job 1 we gleaned many facts about Job, his possessions, and his family. We now come to the next seven verses of the chapter and learn even more about Job and about the enemy of his soul.

10. Read Job 1:6. Where was Satan when he is first mentioned in this book?

In heaven

Some often ask where this meeting took place, and many assume it was in heaven. But why do we know this is wrong? It is because no sin or evil can enter the threshold of God's dwelling place (Psalm 11:4). Therefore the old liar and wicked one cannot enter heaven (Revelation 21:27). does not apply ~ The new Jerus.

[margin note: Not applic. here]

11. What question did God ask the enemy in Job 1:7?

Where do you come from

Since He is our all-knowing God, for whom did He ask it?

the reader

What answer did Satan give to God's question?

From roaming about on the earth

Centuries later, Peter gave a similar description in 1 Peter 5:8 of the evil one's work: "Your adversary the devil, as a roaring lion, walketh about, seeking whom he may devour."

As we will see from the next several verses, Satan had been spending a lot of time in Uz. He had been "going to and fro" around Job's property. He knew about his family, and his great possessions. Only God is all-knowing, but Satan and his demons spend a lot of time observing people who love and serve God.

12. In Job 1:8, God brought up this prince of the East to Satan, the Prince of Darkness. How did God describe His servant once again in this verse?

    Blameless, upright, fearing God—turning away from evil

13. In verse 8 God gave an honorable title to Job when He called him "my servant." What a title of supreme honor for any believer! Several great men in the Bible share this title with Job. Find them in the following verses:

    2 Kings 10:10

    Elijah

    Psalm 105:42

    Abraham

    Isaiah 37:35

    David

    Isaiah 48:20

    Jacob

    Romans 1:1

    Paul

    James 1:1

    Same

    2 Peter 1:1

    Peter

Revelation 1:1

John

Although the accuser found fault with Job, God did not.

14. In Job 1:9–11 what cynical accusations did Satan make against God's servant?

That Job loved God because of God's blessings & protection.

"Satan's accusation of Job was really an attack on God. We might paraphrase it like this: 'The only reason Job fears You is because You pay him to do it. You two have made a contract, You protect him and prosper him as long as he obeys You and worships You. You are not a God worthy of worship! You have to pay people to honor You'"[3]

15. Throughout the Bible we are warned about being ignorant of the wicked one and his hatred of those who are godly. Look up the following verses and record the descriptions given of Satan. _means adversary_

Matthew 13:39

enemy

John 8:44

murderer & liar

2 Corinthians 4:4

god of this world who blinds

1 Peter 5:8

adversary - lion looking to devour

1 John 2:13

evil one

Revelation 12:10

accuser

"All who belong to the Lord Jesus Christ get the special attention of Satan. He watches us very closely . . . assessing our strengths and weaknesses as he devises the best form of attack to bring us crashing down morally and spiritually. And when the time is right, he will strike just as he did with Job."[4]

16. What commandments regarding this enemy are given to us in James 4:7 and 1 Peter 5:9?

Resist him

What provisions for resisting him are given to all believers in Ephesians 6:10–18?

the armor of God · the sword of the spirit,
breastplate of rightousness, shield of faith, helmet
of salvation, girded with truth, prep. of the Gospel

17. What is the certain doom of the "old serpent"? See Revelation 20:10.

the lake of fire

18. Read Job 1:12. How did God allow Satan to test Job's faith?

he could go after everything Job had, but
Job himself

What permission was he given?

What permission did God not give?

We end our first lesson with Satan leaving the presence of the Lord, headed full speed for Uz. As you think about Job 1:6–12, does it seem that Satan was in control of this entire scene? Right here at the beginning, let's establish that God was in complete charge of the meeting described in these seven verses. Satan had to get permission from God to touch His servant Job. In this great book, this is the first appearance of the sovereignty of God. We are reminded here, and throughout Job, that God was indeed reigning over every moment of Job's life. But if that is so, you may ask, why was the greatest man on the earth turned over to the testings of the wicked one? For the answer to that question, we will need to consider carefully the remaining 1,062 verses of this oldest of books.

The Glory of God)

❈❈❈❈❈ TIMELY TRUTHS TO REMEMBER ❈❈❈❈❈

🦋 Twice in these few verses God described Job's testimony of godliness. How would God describe your spiritual life?

How would your pastor describe your walk with God?

How would your husband and children describe your walk with Him?

We may hide our true spiritual condition from others, but not from our all-knowing God.

🦋 If you are a child of God by faith in His Son, Jesus Christ, are you serving Him? Why do you serve Him? Satan said Job served God because God bribed him to do so through His faithfulness and blessings to him. Are you serving out of love and obedience to Him, or for gain and blessing you hope to receive?

🦋 It is sad that so many today who name His name have little interest in serving Him. They have not followed Jesus' instruction in Matthew 6:24 ("No man can serve two masters"), and their thoughts, time, and efforts are spent serving self and this world's system. We are glad for the example of Bible men like Joshua, who openly declared that he and his house would serve God (Joshua 24:15).

The great reformer, Martin Luther, was well-acquainted with the workings of the wicked one. His was a continual battle against the Prince of Darkness and his evil activities during Luther's lifetime (1483–1546). In the following poem he writes of his great God and his great enemy. His words have become one of our most beloved hymns. We end this lesson with his insightful and inspiring words. May we rejoice in the evil one's certain doom and the power of our God to destroy him forever.

A mighty fortress is our God,
A bulwark never failing;
Our helper He, amid the flood
Of mortal ills prevailing.
For still our ancient foe
Doth seek to work us woe;
His craft and pow'r are great,
And, armed with cruel hate,
On earth is not his equal.

And though this world, with devils filled,
Should threaten to undo us,
We will not fear, for God hath willed
His truth to triumph through us.
The prince of darkness grim—
We tremble not for him;
His rage we can endure,
For lo, his doom is sure,
One little word shall fell him.

RESPONDING TO SORROW

"The Lord gave, and the Lord hath taken away." (Job 1:21)

SCRIPTURE TO READ: Job 1:13–2:8

Our first visit to Uz in lesson 1 introduced us to Job, his family, and his prosperity. We learned that he not only prospered financially but also was rich in his walk with God. The Holy Spirit carefully recorded Job's spiritual character not once but twice. In this lesson we find Job's godliness described for us yet a third time. God Himself records that Job was a model servant and that spiritual strengths like his were not found in any other man living at that time.

Because Job faithfully walked with God, and led his family to do the same, why then did the unbelievable events of this lesson come upon him? The fact that even the most godly men and women suffer is one of the major themes woven throughout this ancient book. While suffering is not the main theme of Job, it is certainly an important one. Along with this truth, we also learn from Job the importance of having a right response to our suffering. This lesson, along with lesson 3, will cover wonderful words of submission from the mouth of Job.

Satan also appears in this lesson. His cruelty is pictured here as he carried out his destruction of every material possession Job had. Perhaps his greatest wickedness came when he oversaw the deaths of Job's children and then inflicted unbelievable torment to the body of grieving Job. May this lesson remind us how the king of darkness despises those who love and follow the Light of the World. May we also remember that without the permission of our loving heavenly Father, Satan cannot harm us in any way.

1. Read Job 1:13–17. Describe the great losses Job suffered through the work of the wicked one.

_____

_____

"The repetitive phrase 'While he was still speaking', means not only that he was given no respite but that Satan was determined to bludgeon him into the ground."[1]

2. According to Job 1:18–19, what was the greatest heartache suffered by Job and his wife?

_____

3. What was Job's response to all these horrific losses (Job 1:20–21)?

_____

4. If God took away all you value and love, would you fall down and worship Him? How do you think you would respond? What kind of response would you wish to have?

_____

_____

Job 1:20–22 opens to us one of the most sacred scenes in the book of Job. We need to stand awhile in the shadow of these verses and meditate on what we see and hear. Many valuable lessons are to be learned here about trusting and submitting to our righteous God even in what may be our darkest hour.

5. Job didn't shake his fist at God in anger; instead he reached out his hand and clung to Him in his darkness. What words in 1:20–21 touch your heart most?

_____

_____

6. What does it mean to "charge God foolishly" (1:22)?

_____

_____

Have you ever thought God made a mistake in His dealings with you or another believer? In all of his unimaginable grief Job did not say, "Why me, God?" Nor did he say, "As a godly man I don't deserve such treatment. This is not right!" We do not find that he spoke of these horrible events as mistakes God could have prevented. Job believed God was righteous.

7. God's righteousness is displayed for us throughout Scripture. What did David say about this important subject in Psalm 145:17?

_____

_____

How do Daniel's words in Daniel 9:14 agree with what David said?

_____

_____

It is Thy hand, my God,

My sorrow comes from Thee.

I bow beneath Thy correcting Rod;

'Tis love that bruises me.

~Author unknown

8. Job 2 removes us temporarily from Job's sorrow to yet another meeting with Satan in the presence of God. Describe the scene in 2:1.

_____

_____

9. What words did God use to show His confidence in His servant (2:3)?

_____

_____

_____

10. Read 2:4–5. What was Satan's new charge against Job?

_____

11. In Job 2:6, what permission did our righteous and loving God now give to the wicked one?

_____

_____

12. With what new cruel torments did Job's accuser afflict him (2:7)?

_____

_____

Job's condition

> has been diagnosed variously as boils, leprosy, and more
> likely, elephantiasis. The symptoms given in the book [of
> Job] include the following: aching, rotting bones (30:17),
> dark and peeling skin (30:30), wart-like eruptions (7:5), an-
> orexia (19:20), fever (30:30), depression (7:15–16, 30:15–16),
> weeping (16:16), sleeplessness (7:4), nightmares (7:14), pu-
> trid breath (19:17), failing vision (16:16), and rotting teeth
> (19:20).[2]

13. Read Job 2:8. Where was God's servant Job after Satan afflicted him?

_____

Because of the vicious cruelty of the wicked one, what was this great man doing?

_____

No longer in his master bedroom, or able to have a clean hospital bed, he suffered alone at the town dump. He had no medicine and nothing to relieve his suffering. It was painful to look at him, to smell him, to see the ravages of his disease take their course. Surely his wife would come to comfort him and pour oil into his countless sores, wouldn't she? Yes, she did come to the ash pile to visit him, but we will deal with that encounter in the next lesson.

14. Read Psalm 55. Here we find another godly man, King David, down in the royal dump, sitting on the ashes and crying out to God. What was his cry in 55:1–2?

_____

Whom did David say was responsible for his being down in the dump (55:3)?

_____

Describe his physical and emotional feelings (55:4–5).

_____

_____

How did David want to solve his great problem (55:6–8)?

_____

_____

Why was this wrong?

_____

_____

15. When we are sometimes down at the dump, sitting on our own pile of ashes, what lessons can we learn from David? Read 55:16–17.

_____

_____

_____

16. In Psalm 55:22, what command is given to every child of God?

_____

_____

17. Two promises follow this command in verse 22. What are they and why should they be precious to every believer?

_____

_____

_____

_____

🦋 When faced with trials, disappointment, and sorrows, we, like Job, need God's wisdom and power to have a faith response. Our sinful nature will lead us to thinking like that of Mrs. Job. Jim Berg in his book *When Trouble Comes* says that when "someone is 'living after the flesh' (Romans 8:5), he is handling life the way he wants to handle it, instead of handling life the way God wants it handled."[3] Job put his grief into God's hands, while Job's wife took matters into her own hands. Job rightly called his wife a foolish woman.

🦋 What faith responses have you seen from other believers that have been a blessing to you? Job's faith response in these early chapters of the book bearing his name has been an example to believers for centuries. We learn from him what true godliness looks like when surrounded by howling storms.

🦋 "Satan would have us believe that God is not fair, yet we seldom consider the cruelty of the devil. [He] is as cruel as possible to the saints. . . . When God committed into Satan's hand all of Job's wealth and his children, Satan did not take away just ten per cent: he viciously took it all away and killed every one of Job's children. . . . When the devil learned that he had control of Job's body, he afflicted him not with a common cold or a mild allergy, but with a severely painful disease over his whole body . . . it is clear that Satan would have murdered Job if given the opportunity."[4]

🦋 Do you know someone who is presently sitting on his own ash pile? (Perhaps you are that person!) As we close this lesson, may I leave you with comforting salve for your soul? Unlike poor Job, we have the comfort of the Scriptures (Romans 15:4), where we can pillow our heart. My prayer is that you will turn to the following passages, and allow God to pour comfort into your aching wounds and revive your soul.

Psalm 34:17–19

Psalm 46:1, 10

Isaiah 40:28–31

Isaiah 41:10, 13

Isaiah 43:1–2

I need Thy presence every passing hour;
What but Thy grace can foil the tempter's power?
Who, like Thyself, my guide and stay can be?
Through cloud and sunshine, Lord, abide with me.

~Henry F. Lyte

JOB'S VISITORS

"Shall we receive good at the hand of God, and
shall we not receive evil?" (Job 2:10)

SCRIPTURE TO READ: Job 2:9–13

Satan spared only one of Job's family members—his wife. In her grief she came to the dump to visit Job. Sadly, she became another of Satan's instruments to discourage him because we see that her response to the disasters allowed by God was not one of faith. While her husband had a faith response, she had a faith collapse. We learn this from the only two verses given to her until she is referenced in the last chapter of the book. In just ten words the Holy Spirit reveals to us the spiritual weakness of Job's wife. Her ten-word suggestion to her miserable, afflicted husband are certainly shocking when compared to the earlier compelling words of Job.

Job also had other visitors to his ash pile. In chapter 2, his friends walked onto the stage of this drama, having heard the news of the great disasters that struck their friend, the greatest man in the east.

After they received the news, they began immediately to make plans to visit Job. They cared enough to go without being asked to do so. They did it out of love and concern for their grieving friend.

Many chapters in the book of Job are given to the seemingly endless words of these friends. In this lesson they are speechless, but we will soon see that they had definite ideas as to why Job was suffering so severely. But during this initial visit their sympathy seemed to be genuine, and we can learn several truths from their display of sympathy that will enable us to be better comforters. Just as we learn from Job the right response to our suffering, we learn from these friends the biblical response we are to have to others when they are suffering.

1. Read Job 1:2–5. What blessings had Job's wife experienced because of her godly husband?

_____

_____

_____

Imagine being married to a man about whom God said, "There is none like him in the earth" (1:8; 2:3)! If you are married to a man who walks faithfully with God, give thanks. Like Mrs. Job, you are also a privileged woman.

2. In 2:9, what question did she ask Job? What do you think this means?

_____

_____

3. According to 2:9, what did she tell her disease-stricken husband to do?

Is this strange advice for a wife to give? Explain.

_____

_____

_____

4. Do you think that perhaps she intended to follow her own advice, cursing God and then taking her life? Why or why not?

_____

_____

5. Her harsh and angry words surely rubbed salt into Job's countless boils. Instead of words that hurt, what might she have said that would have encouraged Job?

_____

_____

_____

_____

Perhaps words that assured Job of her love and concern or promises to stay beside him in his suffering would have assuaged his grief. Sadly there are no other recorded visits of Job's wife to the dump during the estimated year of her husband's suffering. We see her again in Job 42. In that setting she surely blushed when she thought of her earlier words to her husband. The God she was quick to blaspheme was faithful to watch over and care for her while her husband suffered on the ash pile.

> As the roots of a tree are tested for strength in a storm, so the storms of sorrow and unexplainable experiences uncover the life foundation of a man. Job had a strong foundation in God; his wife did not. Their different responses to the situation were not due to the way they each experienced the sorrow, but to their foundation.[1]

6. In that ancient culture Job's wife could not turn in her Bible to wonderful verses that proclaimed there is always hope when we

know and trust our God. List four or five of your favorite verses to share with those who might need hope.

_____

_____

_____

_____

7. According to Job, what kind of woman had his wife become since the disastrous events recorded earlier? Read 2:10. What do you think this verse means?

_____

_____

_____

"The word foolish (*nabal*) does not denote a dolt but someone who knowingly rejects the words and ways of God. [Job's] rebuke implies that such language was out of character for her, but in this instance she is thinking like a fool."[2]

8. Have you, or someone you know, ever "charged God foolishly" during times of sorrow? Explain.

_____

_____

_____

_____

What foolish words might people use to curse or blaspheme God for changes that come suddenly into their lives?

_____

_____

Someone has said that the life changes associated with severe trials can either make or break a marriage.

9. Do you agree with the above statement, and can you give some examples you know where this was proven to be true?

_____

_____

_____

_____

In our times of grief we can, like Job's wife, curse God and wither spiritually. Or, like Job, we can submit to God and grow spiritually.

10. Read 2:10 again. From Whose hand do we receive good things? From this same loving hand, what else does Job say we sometimes receive?

_____

_____

_____

Often in Scripture we are reminded that "all things," good or hurtful, come into our life because God allows them. He is always in charge of each event in our life, and He will not fail to help and sustain us. Job knew and submitted to the sovereignty of God in his life. His testimony was similar to that of Victorian hymn writer Anne Cousin, when she penned these comforting words in her great hymn "The Sands of Time Are Sinking."

> With mercy and with judgment
> My web of time He wove,
> And aye the dews of sorrow
> Were lustered by His love.
> I'll bless the hand that guided,
> I'll bless the heart that planned,

When throned where glory dwelleth
In Immanuel's land.

Job, while sitting on ashes, hurting, isolated, and in great misery, still did not make foolish statements against God.

11. What testimony did the Holy Spirit record about Job in the words of 2:10?

_____

_____

_____

It is thought that several weeks elapsed between verses 10 and 11 of chapter 2. Job sat alone at the dump, scraping his sores with someone's broken pottery, wondering if his pain would ever stop. Unknown to Job, the news of his sorrow had traveled quickly, and some of his friends were hurriedly making their way to Uz. Their appearance at the town dump was another of several moving scenes in Job. To close this lesson, we want to draw closer to Job's ash pile and watch as his three friends enter this real-life drama.

12. Read 2:11. Who were the three friends who took time to visit their pitiful friend?

_____

13. For what two reasons had they come to Uz?

_____

14. Read 2:12. What were their reactions as they got close enough to see this friend who was once known as the greatest man in the east?

_____

_____

15. Read 2:13. In what ways did these men show their sorrow for their friend?

_____

_____

_____

16. How might speaking verses like Romans 8:28, for example, actually be hurtful to a believer who is deep in grief?

_____

_____

_____

Like Job's friends, we should faithfully visit the sick and sorrowing. We are commanded to take time to show Christian love and concern. We need to resist the temptation to "sermonize when we've come to sympathize."[3]

17. What do you think it means to "sermonize when we've come to sympathize"?

_____

_____

_____

The comfort of the Scriptures is surely needed for wounded hearts. Without sermonizing, what verses of comfort do you like to share when you visit hurting friends?

_____

_____

_____

Pastor J. H. Jowett (1864–1923) said, "God does not comfort us to make us comfortable, but to make us comforters."[4]

18. Job's friends began as true comforters. Read Job 16:2. As their time at the dump passed, what kind of comforters did they eventually become?

_____

_____

The next several chapters of Job will show us how these men certainly earned such a title! Perhaps we need to ask ourselves: "Would any of my friends call me a miserable comforter?"

※※※※ TIMELY TRUTHS TO REMEMBER ※※※※

 In Psalm 103:10, we read these wonderful words: "For he hath not dealt with us after our sins, nor rewarded us according to our iniquities." I have turned to this verse on many occasions after having my own faith collapse. Aren't we thankful for the mercies of God, which give all of us a second chance? In Job 42, Job's wife received a second chance. As a humbled helpmeet she was glad that her husband did not follow her ungodly counsel to "curse God, and die."

 God's twice-repeated question to Satan was "hast thou considered my servant Job?" (1:8; 2:3). In this lesson we have been considering Job's wife and how she dealt with her overwhelming losses. A poet of the past who spent time considering her penned the following poem.

HAST THOU CONSIDERED JOB'S WIFE?

"Curse God, and die," Job's wife advised,
Her heart o'erwhelmed with strife
When trouble came.
Whom did she blame?
"Curse God and end your life."

Her home and luxuries were gone.
She placed the blame on God.

She did not know
While here below
We need His chast'ning rod.

Impatient with her patient Job,
Resentful of his trust.
Though robbed of health, and all his wealth
Yet love his God he must.

~Esther Archibald[5]

COMFORTERS NEEDED

"Comforters Needed!" could be the advertisement put at the bottom of every church's prayer list. Poor Job needed comforters to stop by his ash pile with cups of cold water and encouraging words. The following ideas have been shared with me by several families who are acquainted with grief and were blessed to be surrounded by caring friends who ministered to them.

Comforters should be sympathizers and not sermonizers. Remember this truth: "When grief is freshest, words should be the fewest." Choose to use verses from Scripture that remind the hurting one of God's abiding love and care.

A sacrifice of time, and perhaps tears, is involved when visiting the sorrowing. It costs to comfort. Consider how far Job's friends traveled to visit him at the dump and their obvious grief when they first saw him. They spent almost a year with him. Later we will see that they were still with him when God brought this story to an end.

As friends go through cancer treatments, recover from a stroke, adjust to the loss of a loved one, learn to attend church services by themselves, or pick up the pieces of broken dreams, they need comforters. Your presence, continual assurance of prayers, and encouraging words will, no doubt, be needed for many months.

"Do not quote Romans 8:28 to a suffering saint. It is a wonderful verse, but the afflicted have thought of that verse long before you have. . . . Sufferers [do draw] comfort from [this verse] but it is not to be doled out like spiritual aspirin, as though it instantly . . . heals all hurts."[6]

A comforter's life must display a message of hope and confidence in God and His wonderful promises. A comforter must know where to find God's promises! What are your favorite promises God has used to comfort you? Keep a list of the great promises where they can easily be found, and look for opportunities to share them.

Take a portable CD player to an invalid's hospital room, along with several sacred CDs. You can encourage the patient and focus his heart on God through the words of the hymns.

Little acts of kindness can mean so much to a sorrowing family. Surprise gifts of stamps, note cards, gum, snacks, devotional books, Scripture plaques, and money all come in handy for those spending long hours at the hospital.

Offers to take family members out for coffee or a meal are welcome. Help by bringing meals or desserts to the home. Keep in mind the size of the family as you prepare meals. Large portions can overload a refrigerator. Bringing food in disposable containers is helpful.

When children or grandchildren are involved with a long family illness or funeral, invitations for childcare can be a great blessing. Inviting them out for treats or play time can also be much appreciated by the children and their parents.

Remember to also comfort the family members of the afflicted (children, grandparents, married children, etc.). They, too, are hurting and need encouragement. Job's wife could have used a comforter. Where were her friends and relatives during her time of grief?

Restaurant and grocery store gift cards are a blessing to those who may be entertaining out of town relatives or friends.

After the funeral or illness is past, let those involved know that you are still thinking about their family. They will never forget the date their loved one died, and it will mean so much to know you haven't forgotten either. A good way to remember is to note the death date on your calendar so that you can send a card when the early anniversaries of their death comes around.

Remembering the family during holidays is a loving way to say you care. The first holidays without loved ones can be very difficult. Christmas, birthday, and Valentine cards to those who have lost loved ones or spouses are encouraging.

Don't remove the family or individual from your prayer list. If we would be a comforter, we must continue to spend time in prayer for those who hurt, and our prayers must be more than "Bless my friend." Get hold of the promises of God for your friend and tell her which promise(s) you are claiming for her. Write these promises on note cards and include them in regular cards of encouragement sent to those needing encouragement.

"A word [of comfort] spoken in due season, how good is it!"

Proverbs 15:23

JOB'S FAINTING FIT

"Let the day perish wherein I was born." (Job 3:3)

<small>SCRIPTURE TO READ: Job 3</small>

I've never heard anyone say Job 3 is his favorite chapter in the Bible. Neither have I known anyone who took a life verse from there or memorized portions of chapter 3; have you? After Job's great statements of faith in the first two chapters of Job, we are not ready for the dark words he speaks in chapter 3. As a matter of fact, I've found his words to be very painful reading. They are mournful and full of longings for death. No wonder Job 3 doesn't top the list of favorite chapters in the Bible!

What happened between Job's great words in 2:10 and those we find in Job 3:1–26? For one thing, time had passed and his grief and pain had, no doubt, increased. Long days and nights on top of an ash pile led him to be weak with weariness. His life was changed forevermore, he thought. But perhaps the worse thing of all was the silence of God. In past days he had walked and talked with God, but many days had passed since those happy meetings. How Job longed to be assured by his Best Friend that all was well. When no such assurance came, Job cried out with death wishes. He was lonely for his God and would rather die than live without Him.

Let's open now the twenty-six verses of Job 3. Yes, Job's words are painful. They are also profitable and full of precious truths for us. Along with Job's friends, we now draw nearer to his ash pile. May the Holy Spirit help us "behold wondrous things" (Psalm 119:18) from this portion of His Word.

> Lord, Thou hast suffered, Thou dost know
> The thrust of pain, the piercing dart,
> How wearily the wind can blow
> Upon the tired heart.
>
> ~Amy Carmichael[1]

1. Read 3:1–3. Job did not yield to his wife's faithless suggestion to curse, or despise, God, but what did he curse in these verses?

In earlier years, Job had undoubtedly rejoiced and celebrated when another birthday rolled around. Now he requested that his birthday be erased from the calendar. No more birthday cards for Job! His life was not worth celebrating.

2. In Acts 17:24–25 we are reminded of the origin of life. As he spoke to the arrogant Greek philosophers, whom did Paul say is the giver of "all life, and breath, and all things"?

God alone had overseen Job's birth in that ancient land. Job had no choice in the matter. God had given Him the breath of life and strength to live and breathe for many years, and God alone could stop his life. As we read Job 3, "We should especially note the patience and long-suffering of God as He responds to Job's outbursts with silence."[2]

3. Read 3:4–10. What additional words of unhappiness did Job pronounce here?

_____

_____

Have you ever been in such emotional distress that you thought it would be better if you had never been born? Author J. Vernon McGee said, "I'm of the opinion that many of us have said it, especially when we were young and something disappointed us. . . . This attitude never solves any problems of this life . . . you simply can't undo the fact that you have been born!"[3]

4. Jeremiah expressed the same regret Job did. Read Jeremiah 20:14–18. What did he write about his birthday?

_____

_____

Both Job and Jeremiah were sorrowing saints. Jeremiah had preached God's truth faithfully, but his people rejected him and God's message. Both of these Bible giants had walked close to God for years, and they both came to doubt in the dark what they had known well in the light. Now they were sorrowing because they thought God had removed His blessing from them, and this thought led them to wish they had never been born. "It is not merely the affliction itself that Job finds so hard to bear, it is the sudden . . . change in God's posture toward him. . . . How can anyone endure such disaster and not assume that God has turned against him?"[4]

Job and Jeremiah felt God had left them. They wrongly believed that His silence meant He was absent. Without His presence and fellowship here on earth, these godly men expressed the wish for a heavenly home. But, will God ever leave His children?

5. What sure words of promise does He give us in the following verses?

Deuteronomy 31:6

_____

Psalm 9:10

_____

Psalm 37:25

_____

Isaiah 49:15

_____

Hebrews 13:5

_____

We need not fear that He will ever leave us. Our greatest fear should be that we will leave Him!

> Prone to wander, Lord, I feel it,
> Prone to leave the God I love;
> Here's my heart, O take and seal it;
> Seal it for Thy courts above.
>
> ~Robert Robinson

6. Read Job 3:11–16. In these verses, what "why" questions did Job have for God?

_____

_____

"There is nothing wrong with asking why, as long as we don't get the idea that God owes us an answer. [Believers] are to live on promises, not explanations."[5] In the book of Job there are almost three hundred questions. Very few, if any, were ever answered by God, and in the end, God had lots of unanswerable questions for Job!

7. Give some "why" questions present-day believers may struggle with? Are you struggling with such questions yourself? Explain.

_____

_____

_____

_____

When we ask God why He allowed some sorrow, loss, or physical problems to come into our lives, what are we saying about our God? Are we insinuating He has made a mistake, is not in charge, or is not fair?

8. What are the commands given to believers in Proverbs 3:5?

_____

_____

When we question God about our trials, are we following these commands? Explain.

_____

_____

_____

_____

Job struggled with why he was born, and why God did not allow him to die at birth. Of course he was speaking of his physical birth. In John 3, Jesus spoke of the need for a second birthday.

9. Read John 3:3, 7. What does it mean to be born again?

_____

_____

How are we born again? Read John 3:14–18.

_____

_____

Have you experienced this new birth by faith in Jesus Christ?

_____

When did you make this important decision in your life?

_____

_____

Our spiritual birthday is one we should always remember and give praise to our God that we are forever His child.

10. Reread Job 3:3, 16. What words here are used by Job to describe unborn children?

_____

Job was declaring, without the advantage of modern-day technology, that he was a real person from the moment of conception.

11. How do rebellious, sinful people in our day often describe unborn children?

_____

How do Job 3:3, 16 refute their assertions?

_____

_____

12. How does Job describe life after death in Job 3:13, 17–19?

_____

_____

While Job longed for the peacefulness of death, he would not experience it for a very long while. Turn to Job 42:16. After his months of suffering, how many more years did God see fit to keep Job from the bliss of heaven?

_____

_____

13. Read Job 3:25–26. For many years Job had lived happily in peace and prosperity. What fear had he carried with him during those times?

_____

_____

14. Do you have similar fears? Have you ever lain awake at night worrying about the loss of health or a job or those you love? Do you think such worry is sin? Explain.

_____

_____

_____

_____

Ye fearful saints, fresh courage take;
The clouds ye so much dread
Are big with mercy, and shall break
In blessings on your head.

Judge not the Lord by feeble sense,
But trust Him for His grace;
Behind a frowning providence
He hides a smiling face.

~William Cowper

As Job spoke the mournful words found in Job 3, his friends were listening to those words.

15. What might they have been thinking about his spiritual condition? (The chapters ahead of us will make plain their conclusions regarding Job's walk with God!)

_____

_____

16. If you heard a friend speak words similar to Job's, what would you say to her?

_____

_____

_____

❈❈❈❈ TIMELY TRUTHS TO REMEMBER ❈❈❈❈

🦋 After reading through this bleak chapter, we may be thinking that perhaps this greatest man in the east wasn't so great after all. But remember Who wrote the words we find in Job 1:1; 1:8; 2:3. Reread God's testimonials for His perfect and upright servant, and remember God is all-knowing (Hebrews 4:13) and He is always right (Psalm 145:17). He knew the heart of His servant and that the affliction He allowed in Job's life would cause him to be an even greater servant.

🦋 Other than our Lord Jesus Christ, perhaps no man ever suffered more than Job. His true story is given that we might have a place to turn when it seems that darkness keeps us from seeing His lovely face and we think we are all alone. I believe Job was lonely for his God. For years, he was on close speaking terms with Him daily, and now the heavens were silent. When we are tempted to think like Job, may we remember that God may be silent, but He is never absent from us. He has promised, and He cannot lie.

🦋 We must not miss in this chapter, and the many that follow, that the book of Job is not just about the suffering of Job. It is mainly about the long-suffering of God for sinful men.

🦋 The book of Job is not just about the patience of Job. (He is not very patient in Job 3, is he?) It is mainly about the patience of God in His dealings with poor sinners like Job—and us.

🦋 Recently I read a story that made me think of Job sitting at the dump wondering the whereabouts of his heavenly Father. Perhaps you will find comfort here for the times you are wondering the same thing.

> The story is told of a little boy who was fearful of going to bed. He was afraid of the dark. Instead of giving him a night-light, his father decided to stay with him in the room, in the dark, until his son fell asleep.
>
> "Are you there, Father?" asked the little boy, with a quiver in his voice.
>
> "Yes, my son," replied the father.
>
> "I can't see your face," said the son.
>
> "But I am looking at you, and I am smiling," the father replied. Then the boy fell asleep. He couldn't see his father, or feel his father's touch, but he heard his father's word, and he believed it and rested in the certainty of it.[6]

When shadows fall and the night covers all,
There are things that my eyes cannot see.
I'll never fear, for the Savior is near;
My Lord abides with me.

When I'm alone and I face the unknown,
And I fear what the future may be,
I can depend on the strength of my Friend—
He walks along with me.

How can I fear? Jesus is near.
He ever watches over me.
Worries all cease;
He gives me peace.
How can I fear with Jesus?[7]

PITY FOR THE PITIFUL

"To him that is afflicted pity should be
shewed from his friend." (Job 6:14)

SCRIPTURE TO READ: Job 4–7

Someone has called Job "the 'logue' cabin of the Bible, con-
structed of four 'logues': a prologue, a dialogue, a monologue,
and an epilogue."[1] Our first four lessons were spent on the prologue.
Our next five lessons will be spent walking through the seemingly
endless dialogue section of the book. Truthfully, these are often the
chapters most of us skip over while hurrying to read Job's happy
ending in the last chapter!

If Job 4–37, the dialogue and monologue chapters, are simply chapters on which believers can practice their speed-reading skills, why
did the Holy Spirit make them the major part of Job's book? Isn't
this also true about major sections of the Old Testament historical
books, and some books of the prophets? Are these somewhat tedious
sections included in the "all Scripture is . . . profitable" statement by
Paul in 2 Timothy 3:16?

We must be careful that we not call unprofitable what God has declared profitable. There is profit for our souls as we wander through this upcoming wilderness of words. This old book of Job is a gold mine for those who take time to dig around in all the veins of its many chapters. I hope you'll stay with us as we continue digging!

Today's lesson introduces us to Eliphaz, probably the oldest of the friends we met in lesson 2. For each of these friends one lesson will be devoted to their first speech, along with Job's answers to their words. For their other dialogues we'll move more quickly, taking time to look at some of the many golden verses sprinkled throughout these chapters. The truths found here will help to encourage and sustain us when trouble comes to our house.

We left a tortured, suffering Job in chapter 3. His condition isn't any better in the chapters before us; in fact, we could say he has moved to the Intensive Care Unit. Into this ICU walks Eliphaz. He heard Job's strong words in chapter 3 and thinks Job is much in need of good spiritual counseling.

1. Read 4:1–4. Eliphaz began with a compliment for the suffering one. What ministries of encouragement was Job known for before his trouble?

_____

2. What accusation did Eliphaz make against Job in 4:5?

_____

Was he calling Job a hypocrite? Explain.

_____

_____

3. Read 4:7–9. What did Eliphaz imply here about Job?

_____

"[Some] talk very glibly about the distrust of those who shrink from every trial; but the man or woman who has suffered much never does this, but is very tender and gentle, and knows what suffering really means."[2]

4. In 4:8 our speaker reminds Job of a great principle found throughout Scripture: a man will reap whatever he sows (Galatians 6:7). When a man is in Job's pitiful condition, does he need such a sermon? Why or why not?

_____

_____

_____

5. Read Proverbs 25:20. How might this verse describe the words of Eliphaz?

_____

_____

6. What helpful commands for encouragers did Paul give us in Romans 12:15?

_____

_____

What are some ways you can follow these commands and encourage someone this week?

_____

_____

_____

We must always remember that right words can be spoken at the wrong time. The men who came to comfort Job had probably suffered very little in their lifetime, and they actually thought their sermons were what sinful Job needed. They insisted on sermonizing instead of sympathizing, insinuating hidden sin in Job's life. Have you ever been tempted to do the same?

7. After a description of his own bone-rattling, hair-raising experience in the past (4:14–15), Eliphaz urged Job to pray (5:1). But what is the big "if" found in his advice?

_____

_____

8. Read 5:4–5. To what grievous events might our speaker have been referring? Why is this like rubbing salt into Job's countless wounds?

_____

_____

Eliphaz continued to weary Job with his nonstop words, always coming back to his theme that unrighteous men suffer and righteous men do not. Of course we have a Bible that says otherwise.

9. Who are the godly men in the verses below who saw great trials as they lived for God and served Him?

Genesis 37:23–27

_____

1 Samuel 18:8–11

_____

Jeremiah 37:13–16

_____

Daniel 6:16–17

_____

10. Read 5:8. To whom did Eliphaz rightly encourage Job to turn for help?

_____

_____

For the next several verses he also encouraged Job to remember the greatness of God.

11. Read 5:9–16. How did Eliphaz describe God and His works?

_____

_____

_____

_____

How did this ancient man know so much about our God?

It [is] clear that families could easily pass down and reinforce important information for many generations. Noah's family carried a tremendous link of traditional knowledge from the old pre-flood world to the new age in which Job and friends lived. . . . But don't forget that God is [also] able to inspire men with unnatural knowledge through His Holy Spirit.³

12. In 5:17–27 what great truths about suffering did Eliphaz speak to weary Job and sufferers of all centuries?

_____

_____

_____

13. Read 5:18 again. What comforting promise is here?

_____

_____

What similar promises did the psalmist make in the following verses?

Psalm 34:18

Psalm 147:3

Are the words of 5:17 and 27 the right words to share with a diseased man in need of critical care? Compare them to the comfort of verse 18. Which would you, as a sufferer, rather hear?

Eliphaz was now finished. Had he brought Job the needed comfort he longed for? We'll find out as we read the fifty-one-verse reply Job gave in Job 6–7.

14. Read 6:1–10. As Job cried out concerning his pitiful situation, whom did he say had afflicted him?

While we know Satan's cruel hand struck Job's family, possessions, and his own body, Who allowed this to happen? See 1:12 and 2:6.

Amy Carmichael, faithful missionary in India for over fifty years, was an invalid for the last twenty years of her ministry. Most of those years she was bedridden, suffering severe pain. Her accident occurred in October of 1931, and in writing of her fall and broken bones she remarked, "The Lord allowed it. Therefore, so far as we are concerned, He did it. Himself hath done it, and all He does is good. And what a special kindness to allow a disablement to come in the direct line of duty. We thank Thee, O Father."[4]

In thinking of the burdens you presently bear, are you willing to give thanks to God and declare that your griefs come from His loving hand?

15. In 6:8–9, what did Job wish for?

_____

_____

Job, Elijah, Moses, and other godly Bible men expressed a wish for death during a time of great grief or stress, but it was a request they left to the will and purposes of God. None took matters into his own hands and attempted to take his life, for life is in the hand of the Giver: "He giveth to all life, and breath, and all things" (Acts 17:25).

16. Read 6:10–14. What kinds of friends did Job wish to have near his ash pile? What is your definition of pity?

_____

_____

_____

17. How have you recently shown true tenderness and understanding for someone who is suffering?

_____

_____

_____

As someone who received great pity from the Savior, Peter commanded believers in 1 Peter 3:8: "Finally, be ye all of one mind, having compassion one of another, love as brethren, be pitiful, be courteous." How has God shown pity for poor, sinful people like us?

_____

_____

18. What do the following verses tell us about compassion to others?

Psalm 103:13–14

_____

Isaiah 63:9

_____

James 5:11

_____

19. In 6:21–30, what further disappointment did Job express about his friends?

_____

_____

20. Read 7:1–6 and describe Job's horrible life as a sufferer at the dump.

_____

_____

_____

His friends went home nightly from the dump, we believe. As wealthy men, they had no doubt traveled to Uz with servants and comfortable living arrangements. Perhaps they had their own tent village somewhere out of the sight and smell of the dump. They had good food to eat and comfortable beds on which to sleep. Did they ever offer to share these comforts with Job? Don't you wish someone could have stood by his ash pile and sung comforting words like these below? Perhaps there is someone you can share them with today.

> Does Jesus care when my heart is pained
> Too deeply for mirth and song;
> As the burdens press, and the cares distress,
> And the way grows weary and long?
>
> O yes, He cares; I know He cares,
> His heart is touched with my grief;
> When the days are weary, the long nights dreary,
> I know my Saviour cares.
>
> ~Frank E. Graeff

In Job 6:7–16 Job expressed further frustration over his situation. He questioned God and his friends in 7:17–21. Job's reply to Eliphaz ended with a pitiful cry that should have moved the heart of his friends to greater pity for him. In our next lesson we will see if the second speaker had kinder words for the man on the ashes. Job no longer needed pity from anyone, but perhaps someone does in your family, church family, or circle of friends. Will you ask God to use the truths we're learning from the book of Job to make you a blessing and comfort to those who are sitting on their modern-day pile of ashes?

✳✳✳✳ TIMELY TRUTHS TO REMEMBER ✳✳✳✳

🕊 Sadly, the men who came to visit Job were themselves part of Satan's plan to defeat and discourage him. We are told in Job 2 that when they began their long journey to Uz, their purpose was to mourn with him and bring comfort. Their motives in coming were excellent, but after seeing the disaster surrounding their friend "they must necessarily have begun to think 'Why has this evil come upon him? God punishes the ungodly; the righteous are prosperous; therefore . . . can it be [that Job is ungodly]?'"[5]

🙶 We must be cautious in coming to false and hurtful conclusions when troubles come into the lives of our friends. Instead, we need to seek ways to encourage them in their troubles. Here are some of the favorite "trouble" verses I've been able to share with friends in need of encouragement. All are from Psalms, and many were written by David, who was himself a frequent resident of the royal dump!

Psalm 9:9

Psalm 27:5

Psalm 46:1

Psalm 86:7

Psalm 119:143

Psalm 138:7

In shady, green pastures so rich and so sweet,
God leads His dear children along;
Where the water's cool flow bathes the weary one's feet,
God leads His dear children along.

Though sorrows befall us and Satan oppose,
God leads His dear children along;
Through grace we can conquer, defeat all our foes,
God leads His dear children along.

Some through the waters, some through the flood,
Some through the fire, but all through the blood;
Some through great sorrow, but God gives a song,
In the night season and all the day long.

~G. A. Young

MORE WORDS AT THE DUMP

"For he breaketh me with a tempest, and multiplieth
my wounds without cause." (Job 9:17)

SCRIPTURE TO READ: Job 8–10

I n this lesson we meet the second of Job's friends. After reading his words, we may think it would have been best if he and
the others had stayed home. While Eliphaz was somewhat tempered
and encouraging in his first words to Job, Bildad was blunt, bold,
and brutal. Such nonsympathizing words are just the kind we all
long to hear when we're suffering, aren't they?

"Sticks and stones may break my bones, but words will never hurt
me" is an old playground rhyme that is untrue. Most of us have
found there are words that cut into our souls very deeply, leaving
behind severe wounds. Job was on the receiving end of such words,
and perhaps the most hurtful thing about this was that the words
came from his friends. Before God brought Job's story to an end, He
would have a few words of His own for Bildad, Eliphaz, Zophar,

and Elihu. But until we reach that part of the story, we must sit together once more at the dump where, it seems, is never heard an encouraging word.

1. Bildad began by commenting on Job's answer to Eliphaz. Read 8:2. What did he say about the words that Job had just spoken?

What a way to encourage a suffering man. Call him a windbag! This fellow was, no doubt, one who believed the little rhyme about words never hurting. A wise Victorian pastor, Charles Spurgeon, once said, "Many persons think they are wise when they are only windy."[1] Surely he was talking about Bildad and friends.

2. Read 8:4. Like Eliphaz in 5:4, Bildad brought up Job's ten dead children. What judgmental insinuation did he make as the reason for their death?

Isn't this like someone standing with grieving parents next to their dead child's casket and reminding them that "the way of transgressors is hard" (Proverbs 13:15)? God doesn't say anything about Job's children being guilty of sin against Him.

3. More low blows are found in 8:5–7. What did Bildad urge Job to do immediately if he would have God's blessing in his life again?

Note 8:6. There is a big "if" at the beginning of this verse. What could Bildad have been implying about Job?

In 8:7, Bildad made a prophecy about Job: "Though thy beginning was small, yet thy latter end should greatly increase." A humbled Bildad would soon see his own prophecy fulfilled before his very eyes!

4. Read 8:11–13. Bildad inflicted yet deeper wounds on Job when he implied Job had forgotten God, and his spiritual roots had withered up due to his sin. What name did he call Job in 8:13?

There is truth in many things Job's friends said, but they were truthful words spoken at the wrong time. Certainly there are many warnings in the Bible about forgetting God and living only for self. When that happens, a believer will indeed wither and die spiritually.

Are you fearful of forgetting God? What have you purposed in your heart to do so that this will not be true in your life? What are some things that will keep you on the path of righteousness?

Read Psalm 106:13, 21. The sad words found here could have been written on the tombstone of God's people, Israel. They could also be written on the gravestones of many in our present age. May it not be so with any who read these words.

5. Bildad had bluntly told Job he needed to repent and seek God (8:5), otherwise he would have no hope (8:14) and no help (8:20). According to 8:7 and 21–22, what would be his reward for repentance?

As mentioned earlier, Bildad would live to see the day Job laughed and rejoiced once again. Could he and his friends be some of those who would be "clothed with shame" (8:22) with little to laugh about on that day?

Job had not laughed for a long time. His only sounds were groans and cries of anguish from the cruel disease inflicted on him by the enemy of his soul. How would Job reply to Bildad? Let's draw closer to the ash pile to hear the words he had for Bildad in Job 9. We also want to hear the words he spoke to God in Job 10, remembering that his words are also for us.

6. What question did Job ask Bildad in 9:2?

_____

_____

Job was not asking here the same question Paul addressed in Romans 3. Paul's teaching spoke of the important truth of how a sinner can be declared righteous before a holy God. Job asked how he could prove to God that he was suffering unfairly, and he desired a chance to prove this before God. He rightly believed he was a righteous man. He wanted an opportunity to plead his case before God (9:3).

7. Read 9:32. Why did Job believe such an opportunity was impossible?

_____

_____

In earlier days Job had faithfully walked and talked with God. He knew firsthand of His power and greatness. He also knew how puny he, a mortal man, was in comparison. Perhaps hymn writer Anna Warner was thinking similar thoughts when she wrote for little children a truth Job had learned centuries earlier: "[I] am weak, but He is strong."

8. Read 9:4–10. List the phrases Job used to describe the character and works of his great God.

_____

_____

_____

Read verse 10 again. The truth stated here is similar to that in 5:9. The Bible is a record of the uncountable wonders God did in Job's life.

9. List some of the wonders He has done for you.

_____

_____

_____

_____

10. Read Psalm 77:10–14. What word do we find repeated three times in verses 10–11?

_____

Why is it so hard to remember the blessings and wonders God showers on us?

_____

_____

_____

11. In verse 12, we read of two helpful things Asaph said to do to remember God's wonders. What are they? When is the last time you did these two things? List several specific ways you can do them today.

_____

_____

_____

_____

12. Asaph spoke again in Psalm 78:10–11. Here he reminded God's people, Israel, of the sins of their fathers. What three sins were they guilty of?

_____

_____

_____

God showed some of His greatest wonders to the children of Israel as He delivered them and led them to the Promised Land. Imagine forgetting the miracles in Egypt, the crossing of the Red Sea, manna from heaven, water from a rock, and so much more! We also forget, do we not? Read the following verse from John Newton's powerful hymn "Great God of Wonders." What did he consider to be God's greatest wonder?

> Great God of wonders, all Thy ways
> Are matchless, God-like, and divine;
> But the bright glories of Thy grace
> Above Thine other wonders shine,
> Above Thine other wonders shine.

For the rest of Job 9, Job spoke to his friends of pleading his cause before God. How he desired to speak with Him as he had in times past!

13. After reading the following verses, describe the suffering Job believed God had allowed to come upon him, an innocent and godly man.

    Verse 17

    _____

    Verse 19

    _____

    Verse 22

    _____

    Verse 25

    _____

    Verse 34

    _____

In Job 10, Job turned his bleary eyes upward in prayer to God. Once again he began with familiar words about his situation. We must be careful about getting impatient with Job, remembering his cry for pity in 6:14: "To him that is afflicted pity should be [shown] from his friend."

14. Read the following verses in Job 10, and write out the cries and requests Job poured out before God. Do any of these sound similar to his words in chapter 3?

Verse 2

_____

Verse 3

_____

Verse 7

_____

Verse 8

_____

Verse 15

_____

Verse 16

_____

Verse 18

_____

Verse 20

_____

15. Read 10:3, 7–8 again. What did Job say about God's hands in these verses?

_____

_____

_____

There are numerous mentions of God's hands sprinkled throughout the book of Job and the entire Bible. It has always comforted me to think of God's hands holding me up. The practice of describing God in human terms has a big theological name: anthropomorphism. While this long word might not just roll off your tongue, you can remember that because God loves us He gives us these human descriptions of Himself so that we might understand all his loving care.

16. What human terms in the following verses describe to us His love and care?

Numbers 6:25

_____

Deuteronomy 33:27

_____

Psalm 8:3

_____

Psalm 8:6

_____

Psalm 31:15

_____

Psalm 34:15

_____

Proverbs 2:6

_____

Isaiah 49:16

_____

Remembering these truths about God will comfort and guide us through our most difficult days. Sharing these truths with hurting friends will also bring new strength to their hearts. What a blessing it would have been to Job if his friends had reminded him of God's strong hands, hearing ears, loving arms, and ever-present eyes, which watched over him day and night.

Unlike Job, the apostle Paul had great friends who comforted him and helped him in the many difficult days he had after becoming a Christian.

17. Read 2 Corinthians 11:24–28. What persecutions and trials from his life did Paul list?

_____

_____

_____

_____

In His mercy, God raised up men and women to help and comfort Paul in his work for God.

18. Read Philippians 4:15–18 and Romans 16:1–9. Who were some of these helpers?

_____

_____

_____

We are thankful to read of God's long-suffering and love for Job as well as His comfort and care for Paul. Such reading never grows old. Think of the countless saints in every century who have read and been reminded that just as God was faithful to these servants, His faithfulness would just as surely surround them. What a wonderful God we serve!

"Neither Job nor Paul ever knew (so far as we know) why prayer for relief was answered as it was. But I think that they must stand in awe, and joy, as they meet others in the heavenly country who were strengthened and comforted by their patience and valor, and the record of their Father's thoughts of peace toward them."[2]

TIMELY TRUTHS TO REMEMBER

- Eliphaz and Bildad brought little comfort to their suffering friend. Should you have had opportunity to sit close to his ash pile, what words of comfort would you have spoken to Job? What truths about God could you have mentioned to encourage him?

- If we are to truly encourage the hurting, we must offer them more than a little pep talk. Such talk flows easily from unbelievers whose only words of comfort may be "hang in there" or "I know your luck will change soon." When we become believers who truly know God, not just about Him, then we will have words that offer hope and encouragement.

- As we end this lesson, we have completed almost one-fourth of the book of Job. The friends who came to "mourn with [Job] and to comfort him" (2:11) were full of countless words. But have you noticed that not one of them mentioned praying for Job? As far as we know, none of them breathed a prayer for their troubled friend in the entire book. Words and advice count for little unless they are supported by faithful prayer.

We may often tell our hurting friends we are praying for them. I believe it's good to also tell them how we're praying for their needs. Here are a few suggestions I often use, and I'm sure you can add several of your own:

- I am praying that your faith will not fail during this difficult time (Luke 22:32).

- I am praying that God will strengthen you, and your family, with new strength in your souls during your days of trial (Psalm 138:3).

- I am praying that you will patiently wait upon the Lord and be of good courage (Psalm 27:14).

- I am praying that God will show you His ways and direct you to the paths He has for you (Psalm 25:4).

- I am praying that He will be your "refuge and strength, a very present help" in your time of trouble (Psalm 46:1).

- I am praying that you will "be still, and know that [He is] God" and that "the Lord of Hosts is with [you]" (Psalm 46:10–11).

> "The Lord God has given me the tongue of the learned, that I should know how to speak a word in season to him that is weary." (Isaiah 50:4)

"YET WILL I TRUST HIM"

"Wherefore hidest thou thy face, and holdest
me for thine enemy?" (Job 13:24)

SCRIPTURE TO READ: Job 11–14

In this lesson another of Job's visitors had his opportunity to "comfort" his ailing friend. After weeks of horrible suffering, and two friends insisting he must repent of his secret sin and get right with God, we are hoping this third man, Zophar, would take pity on the sufferer. Why could he not speak words that would bring healing and hope to his tortured friend? Sadly, Zophar has other words in mind. "The greatest mystery in the book of Job is not why Job suffers, but why a man crippled by suffering is forced to fight a long, drawn out theological battle with people who are supposed to be his friends."[1]

We are only a few words into his speech before we realize Zophar was the least sympathetic of the three visitors! We also see that he was singing the same song as that of his fellow comforters, but his was an even more vicious and pitiless version.

Before you are tempted to leave the ash pile out of impatience with Job's "comforters," let me encourage you to stay put by the ashes. Otherwise, you will miss hearing words from Job that one great preacher of the past called the noblest in the whole record of human speech.

1. Zophar was eager to answer Job's recent barrage of words. Read 11:2–3. What were his opening charges against Job?

   _____

   In 11:4, what specifically did Zophar think Job had lied about?

   _____

2. According to 11:5, what did Zophar desire to hear from the mouth of God?

   _____

   How had God described Job earlier in the book? Read 1:8 and 2:3.

   _____

Job had lost almost everything except his life. But Zophar, who had suffered little and had not one boil on his well-clothed body, thought Job deserved greater punishment (11:6). "Your situation should be even worse, Job. You got off easy!" What a statement from a man whose intention for coming to Uz was "to mourn with [Job] and to comfort him" (2:11)!

3. What name did this cruel comforter call Job in 11:11?

   _____

4. Read 11:13–14. If Job wanted to restore fellowship with his God, what must he do according to Zophar?

   _____

   _____

If Job followed this simple suggestion and turned from his sin, what blessings did Zophar say God would return to Job? See 11:15–19.

_____

_____

5. What is the first word of 11:20? What according to Zophar would be Job's certain doom if he chose to reject Zophar's counsel?

_____

_____

_____

He wrapped up his speech with a vicious attack on a man whom God had announced as the greatest man on the earth (1:8; 2:3). We want to hurry away from a man like Zophar and his attempts to lash Job to death with his tongue.

We want to note here that all three men who spoke did exhibit a knowledge of God. Missing from their speeches, however, were few, if any, words of mercy, pity, and compassion for poor Job. When we have opportunity to visit hurting friends, may we always try to take with us mercy, not misery.

It was Job's time to speak, and he had a mouthful to say to Zophar! Actually, his speech covers seventy-five verses! While we won't study each of these, there are four areas he addressed from which we can profit and receive blessing. Let's look at each of these briefly.

- The blessing of knowing God is sovereign in all our affairs

- The blessing of trusting God

- The blessing of God's face shining upon us

- The blessing of His presence when we are in trouble

6. Before these blessings, however, came a little sarcasm from Job. Read 12:1–3 and 13:2, 4. His impatient tongue had what message for his comforters?

_____

_____

_____

THE BLESSING OF GOD'S SOVEREIGNTY

In 12:7–25, Job spoke eloquently about the power of God in the affairs of all He has created. This is not the last time we'll be treated to his wonderful descriptions of our Almighty God. Job's knowledge of Jehovah God puts many modern believers to shame.

7. To what do the animals, birds, and fish of the earth testify regarding God's creation (12:7–9)?

_____

_____

8. Read 12:10. Who controls the soul and breath of every living thing?

_____

What similar truth is found in 14:5?

_____

_____

9. What is meant when we speak about the "sovereignty of God"?

_____

_____

_____

"Notice that in the heart of the word 'sovereignty' you find the word 'reign.' The sovereignty of God, simply stated, refers to His undisputed authority and rule over every aspect of His creation. God is the great King, the only sovereign over all the earth. No scheme or sin or circumstance takes Him by surprise. No man or demon or force of nature can thwart His power or frustrate His purposes. He alone rules supreme."[2]

> "Thine, O Lord, is the greatness, and the power . . . and the majesty: for all that is in the heaven and in the earth is thine . . . and thou art exalted as head above all." (1 Chronicles 29:11)

10. Read Job 12:13–25. Here is a wonderful exaltation of our sovereign God at work. List the activities of God that Job described in these verses.

_____

_____

_____

_____

> "God is God; He sees and hears
> All our troubles, all our tears.
> Soul, forget not, 'mid thy pains,
> God o'er all for ever reigns."[3]

THE BLESSING OF TRUSTING GOD

11. What well-known cry from Job's heart is found in Job 13:15? Write out the verse.

_____

_____

This cry is not the utterance of any commonplace believer. If he died on the ash pile, Job said he would die trusting his God.

12. In your own words, what does it mean to trust, or have faith, in God?

_____

_____

_____

Give something specific you are presently trusting Him to do in your life.

_____

_____

_____

What is the source of our faith? See Romans 10:17.

_____

Why is faith important for a believer? Read Hebrews 11:6.

_____

_____

Many people in the Bible have expressed words similar to those of Job in 13:15. Habakkuk was one man who did.

13. How are Habakkuk's words in Habakkuk 3:17–18 similar to Job's?

_____

_____

In our darkest hours, will we trust Him? When all around us is failing, and there seems to be no hope, will we trust Him? Will we keep waiting, knowing that our God indeed reigns over our situation whether or not we can see it? What great words are these in Job 13:15! And to think they came from the diseased lips of a poor saint sitting on a pile of ashes. "Perhaps the reason why God is trusted so little, is because He is so little known . . . if we knew Him more, we would trust Him more."[4]

Trust Him when dark doubts attack thee,
Trust Him when thy strength is small,
Trust Him when to simply trust Him
Seems the hardest thing of all.

~Lucy Bennett [5]

THE BLESSING OF HIS FACE SHINING UPON US

Job spoke to God in Job 13:20–14:22. His desire to have fellowship once again with God was evident throughout these verses. While we will not look at every verse, there are some we must not hurry over without a closer look.

14. What question did Job have for God in 13:24?

Do you remember the term for describing God in human terms, i.e., His hands, ears, arms, and so forth? See lesson 6 for the answer.

In 13:20–24, Job said he hungered to fellowship with God once again. He stated he had never hidden from God (verse 20), and he was greatly grieved that God had become a stranger to Him. How he valued his close walk with God. May it be the same with us!

15. In 13:24, Job sought God's face. What does this mean?

16. What has God promised His children in Hebrews 13:5 and Deuteronomy 31:6?

How can we sometimes separate ourselves from His presence and blessing? Read Isaiah 59:2 to find the answer.

_____

_____

_____

17. Since our sins cause Him to hide His face from us, what must we do to have His face shine on us once again? See 1 John 1:9, Psalm 38:18, and Psalm 51:3.

_____

_____

18. The writers of the psalms often referred to the face of God. In the following verses, what do their prayers express about His face?

Psalm 27:7–9

_____

Psalm 67:1

_____

Psalm 102:2

_____

Psalm 119:135

_____

These are great prayers for us to meditate on and to include in our own times of prayer.

> I take, O cross, thy shadow
> For my abiding place;
> I ask no other sunshine than
> The sunshine of His face;
> Content to let the world go by,

To know no gain nor loss,

My sinful self my only shame,

My glory all the cross.

~Elizabeth Clephane

THE BLESSINGS OF HIS PRESENCE
IN OUR TIMES OF TROUBLE

In Job 14:1–12, Job gave us a sobering picture of the fragile life cycle of man. If we summarize these verses, he was saying life is short but it is long on trouble. Many who are reading these words know exactly what Job meant.

19. While there are many joys in our lives, suffering Job told us in 14:1 that life is also full of something else. What is it?

_____

20. David agreed with Job in Psalm 34:19. What did David add to his statement on life that Job didn't?

_____

_____

_____

Undoubtedly some who read these words are presently surrounded with serious troubles. The following are just a few of the countless "trouble verses" He has given for our comfort. Someone has said these promises take on new meaning when read through tear-stained eyes.

Psalm 32:7

Psalm 34:6

Psalm 37:39

Psalm 91:15

✿ "There is no attribute of God more comforting to His children than that of God's sovereignty. Under the most difficult circumstances, in the most severe trials, they believe that the Sovereign One has ordained their afflictions. On the other hand, there is no truth more hated by the world . . . as the sovereignty of our God. Men will allow God to be everywhere except on the throne of their lives."[6]

✿ Is the Sovereign One reigning over your heart today? Are you willing to say with the hymn writer, "Come and reign over me, Ancient of Days"?

✿ In addition to Job's great declaration of faith in Job 13:15, most believers are also acquainted with Solomon's words of faith in Proverbs 3:5–6. As a young believer I was more familiar with Solomon than Job. So when I clipped the following poem from a magazine over forty year ago, I taped it in my Bible alongside Solomon's words. I know nothing of the poem's author, but her words have often encouraged me as I've struggled to trust God instead of trusting my own wisdom. Perhaps the words will bring encouragement to your life too.

I will not doubt, though all my ships at sea
Come drifting home with broken masts and sails;
I shall believe the Hand which never fails,
From seeming evil worketh good to me;
And, though I weep because those sails are battered,
Still will I cry, while my best hopes lie shattered,
"I will trust in Thee!"

~Ella Wheeler Wilcox[7]

WORDS:
WEARY AND WONDROUS

"Open thou mine eyes that I may behold wondrous
things out of thy law." (Psalm 119:18)

SCRIPTURE TO READ: Job 15–21

As we approach these remaining dialogue chapters, you may
be wondering how there can possibly be anything left to dialogue about! Does the thought of covering all these chapters cause
you to be down in the dump yourself? If so, let me encourage you to
knock the dust off these rarely read chapters and find a comfortable
seat close to Job's ash pile. Believe me, there are plenty of wondrous
verses in the chapters before us that you will not want to miss.

As we begin the lesson, will you pray with me the psalmist's prayer
in Psalm 119:18? Will you ask God to open your eyes to behold the
wonderful truths He has placed in this section for us? All the Bible
is wonderful, full of wondrous things, and that even includes chapters 15–21 of Job.

GRACE FOR EVERY TRIAL

1. Job's three friends were ready to preach more sermons to his sore heart. Read the following verses and give the additional charges his friends had for the sufferer.

Eliphaz

Job 15:5

_____

Job 15:13

_____

Job 15:34

_____

Bildad

Job 18:21

_____

Zophar

Job 20:4–5

_____

Job 20:11–12

_____

Do some of these words sound similar to those we have heard before? From the beginning of their speeches the accusations of the three friends rested upon four misconceptions:

(1) The trials are punishment for Job's sins.

(2) The godly do not experience trials.

(3) We can know why God acts as He does toward mankind.

(4) Human history gives us a valid basis for drawing conclusions about trials.

To one degree or another, all these misconceptions are held by Christians today. Our responsibility toward others who may undergo trials is to comfort, not accuse.

2. Look at the four misconceptions once again. Do you agree or disagree with these? Support your answers with Scripture.

3. After sitting through these continual false charges and insults, Job had a few strong words for his friends. What name did he call them in Job 16:2?

_____

One author said they are "comforters who increase trouble instead of ministering comfort."[1] For certain, everyone knows what is meant by "Job's comforters," and it's not a name we want others to call us, is it? Believers should always be merciful comforters, not miserable ones.

4. What are some ways we can be true comforters to the hurting people God brings into our lives?

5. What are some reasons believers may sometimes hesitate to comfort another person who is very ill or has suffered great loss?

_____

_____

_____

Seeing a friend or loved one very ill or distraught can be overwhelming. It may even cause us to keep our distance for fear we won't say the right thing or even make matters worse. God has called us to be comforters, and He has kindly provided in His Word all we need to fulfill this important role.

6. According to 2 Corinthians 1:4 what has God given to every believer to help us to know how to comfort others?

_____

_____

7. Read Job 16:4–5. If the situation were reversed, Job would not have been a miserable comforter to them, he says. What would he have done instead as a merciful comforter?

_____

_____

How can we strengthen others with our mouths?

_____

_____

8. Read Job 16:8. In this verse, what did Job accuse his friends of doing? What does this mean?

_____

_____

Not only was Job's face covered with boils, but added to that ugliness were lots of wrinkles. Job said his friends had taken turns pinching wrinkles on his poor, tired face. Wrinkles are still being pinched on twenty-first century faces, aren't they?

9. How do children pinch wrinkles on their parents' face?

_____

How do parents pinch wrinkles on their child's face?

_____

How do church members pinch wrinkles on their pastor's face?

_____

How can we pinch wrinkles on the faces of our friends?

_____

Has anyone ever pinched wrinkles on your face?

_____

There is no cream at the pharmacy to cure these types of wrinkles. But God's Word brings guaranteed comfort that will replace wrinkles with joy and peace. I have seen wrinkles slowly erased from tired faces when true godly sorrow and repentance are practiced by those who pinched the wrinkles. It is comforting to remember that Job's wrinkles were removed in chapter 42 when God once again brought joy and peace to his life.

We now move from wrinkles to the wicked. Almost half of the words spoken by the "comforters" in chapters 15–21 had to do with wicked men. But it is not just wicked men in general that they described. No, they had one specific man in mind. Can you guess who it might have been?

Eliphaz, Bildad, and Zophar actually had a good understanding of those who were walking in rebellion against God. I believe they were quite proud they were not in that category. However, they were convinced that the man on the ash pile was there because he was indeed wicked.

10. How do the following verses rightly describe a wicked man's life and/or future?

Job 15:25

_____

Job 18:5–6

_____

Job 18:16–17

_____

Job 20:4–5

_____

11. Job also had a few things to say about the wicked. Read his words in Job 21:7–30. In the following verses how did he rightly describe ungodly men?

Job 21:7–13

_____

Job 21:14–15

_____

Job 21:17

_____

12. In Job 21:27 what words did Job have for his accusers?

_____

Wicked hearts have rebelled against their Creator since the Garden of Eden. Throughout Scripture God has given us countless verses describing the work of the wicked person, his hatred of our sovereign God, and his certain doom if he does not turn from his wicked ways.

13. Read Job 21:14–15 again. What is the age-old cry of the wicked?

_____

_____

14. What similar cries and acts of rebellion are recorded in these verses?

Psalm 10:4–15

_____

Psalm 12:4

_____

Romans 1:28–32

_____

15. If rebellious man humbles himself before God, repents, and seeks His mercy, will God save him? Read Romans 10:13 and Hebrews 7:25 to find the answer.

_____

Paul was a rebellious blasphemer who found that our God is great in mercy (1 Timothy 1:12–16). Many of us have friends or family members who say they don't care to know about God. Reading Paul's testimony regularly will encourage us to keep praying for them. God is still able to "save them to the uttermost that come unto God by [Christ]" (Hebrews 7:25).

16. Read Job's words of hopelessness in 19:6–12. According to him, what things had God done to him and his happy life?

_____

17. In Job 19:13–19, what relationship did Job have with relatives, servants, and loving friends of former days?

———————————————————

What cry did he make to these friends and family members in 19:21–22?

———————————————————

Job had been a popular and respected man in Uz. Much of his joy had come from those he wrote of in Job 19. We wonder where these folks were during the long months he spent at the town dump. As far as we can tell, none of them dropped by to encourage him, not even his wife. Why didn't they bring comfort to Job? Perhaps they felt the same way his wordy companions at the dump felt: Job's great sorrow surely was due to great sin.

18. Read Job 19:23–24. Why do you think Job wanted his words of woe to be written and engraved in stone for future generations?

———————————————————

———————————————————

Aren't we glad God answered Job's request? He had no idea his words, and the events of his life, would live forever as a part of God's eternal Word! We are especially thankful for the wondrous words in Job 19:25–27. After all the words about wrinkles and wicked men you have, no doubt, been wondering when we are going to find any words that could be called wondrous. But after many chapters of mostly hopeless words, we suddenly come upon a glorious message of hope.

19. What is the supreme statement of faith Job made in 19:25–27?

———————————————————

———————————————————

What things did he know for certain about his God and his eternal future?

_____

_____

Surrounded by miserable comforters, Job spoke with certainty of the One Who was his merciful comforter. Most of Job's earthly friends had left him, but he had a greater Friend Who would never forsake him. Praise God, we have this same friend if we are His child! Believers for hundreds of years have read Job's wondrous words and received hope.

20. In 1 Corinthians 15:16–19, Paul tells us that without this hope, what is our condition?

_____

"The Christian's promise is that 'if we suffer, we shall also reign with Him' (2 Timothy 2:12). A hope for eternity helps the believer to endure the perplexing problems of life, for the afflictions of this life are only momentary and work for us 'a far more exceeding and eternal weight of glory' (2 Corinthians 4:17)."[2]

> I know that my Redeemer liveth,
> And on the earth again shall stand;
> I know eternal life He giveth,
> That grace and pow'r are in His hand.
>
> I know His promise never faileth,
> The word He speaks, it cannot die;
> Tho' cruel death my flesh assaileth,
> Yet I shall see Him by and by.
>
> ~Jessie Pounds

🦋 We began this lesson with the prayer of the psalmist: "Open thou mine eyes, that I may behold wondrous things out of thy law" (Psalm 119:18). There were many wondrous truths found tucked into all the corners of these seven chapters, if we have eyes to see them. Yes, there are serious lessons to be learned about pinching wrinkles onto the faces of others. And how sobering are the truths about wicked, rebellious man and his future appointment before our Almighty God. While we profit from remembering these, my prayer is that you will not soon forget all the "wondrous things" found in this section of Job's book. The next time you listen to Handel's *Messiah*, and hear the soloist sing the powerful words found in Job 19:25–26, remember that suffering Job first spoke these words while sitting on an ash pile at the dump.

🦋 Reading about the wicked should lead us to pray the words of David in Psalm 139:23–24: "Search me, O God, and know my heart: try me, and know my thoughts: and see if there be any wicked way in me, and lead me in the way everlasting."

🦋 Before the events of Job 1–2, Job had been a loved and respected man in the land of Uz. Much of his joy came from activities with people he mentioned in Job 19:13–22. Now as a tortured, helpless, and lonely resident of the dump, he was learning to do without all these things he had taken for granted in happier days.

🦋 Learning to do without with an attitude of contentment was sometimes irritating to missionary Amy Carmichael. In her book *Rose from Brier* she wrote of things she learned to do without after her serious fall in October 1931.

Suddenly helpless, she wrote of learning to do "without health, without power to go about like others, do simple things, enjoy things without pain, and be in the joyful stream of (ministry) activities. The trial of helplessness [she found] can turn to fierce irritation for one accustomed to paddling her own canoe."[3]

Like Job, and Amy Carmichael, some who read these words are also learning to do without. Perhaps you are a widow learning to do without the company of your spouse, or maybe you are learning to do without a job you depended on, health you once enjoyed, or the company of a beloved friend or family member now in heaven. May our Father, Who comforts us in all the changes of our lives, pour His comfort and contentment into your hurting heart today.

Take your broken dreams upon His holy mountain,
Lay them in His hands and let Him give you peace.
Your help comes from the Lord,
He never slumbers, never sleeps,
Trust in Him, the Keeper of your soul.

Take your broken heart upon His holy mountain,
Lay it in His hands and let your struggles cease.
Like the potter molds the clay,
He can mend and make you whole,
Trust in Him, the Keeper of your soul.

~Barry Lyall and Lew King[4]

"I SHALL COME FORTH AS GOLD"

"My heart standeth in awe of thy word." (Psalm 119:161)

SCRIPTURE TO READ: Job 22–28

*A*wesome is a word often misused today. A football game is awesome as is a new pair of shoes or a good piece of watermelon. We may admire and appreciate these things, but do we truly reverence or stand in wonder of them? That is the meaning of *awe*: a feeling of reverence, fear, and wonder.

King David wrote that his heart stood in awe of God's Word. While he had access only to the earliest books of the Bible, he said that when he read these, or heard them read, he had a feeling of reverence and fear at their majesty and greatness. Although a king surrounded by wonderful things, he said that all these paled in comparison to the wonderful Word of God. What would he have thought of the entire Bible, which is available to us? In our possession and language for hundreds of years now, how often do we reverence it and stand in wonder of its words?

Job is probably the oldest book of the Bible. It contains so many wonderful words that we are staggered by their beauty. We especially stand in awe of the descriptions of our great God. In this lesson we come upon words that are awesome in the truest sense of the word. Verses in Job 26 and 28 remind us again that the greatness of our God is unspeakable (Psalm 145:3)!

As with early patriarchs, Job spoke face to face with God. This continual communication led him to be well acquainted with the Almighty. In Job 23 he stated he had not "gone back from the commandment of his lips: [he had] esteemed the words of his mouth more than [his] necessary food" (Job 23:12). My prayer is that the study of this great man, and the book that bears his name, will cause us to truly stand in awe of the wonderful Word of God and to value it even more than our necessary food.

Before we begin the second half of Job, let's pause to remember the twenty-one chapters we've already covered. What wondrous—and not so wondrous—words we've heard while sitting together at the dump!

1. So far, which verses have meant the most to you? Write several of the references below.

_____

_____

_____

_____

Perhaps you wrote down some of my favorites: 1:21; 2:10; 6:14; 12:10; 13:15; 16:5; and 19:25–27. You can be certain to add many more to the list before we've completed the last twenty-one chapters of the book!

Job 22 and 25 are the last of many finger-pointing lectures from Job's three friends. Our focus in this lesson will be only on Eliphaz's words, as Bildad and Zophar run out of gas with nothing worthwhile left to say!

2. Read Job 22:1–22. What familiar charges against Job are repeated in the following verses?

Job 22:5

_____

Job 22:7–10

_____

Job 22:21–22

_____

3. Read Job 22:23–30. What counsel did Eliphaz give Job in verse 23?

_____

_____

If he did return to the Almighty after confessing his supposed high crimes, what would be the results (22:24–28)?

_____

_____

We find in these verses a true picture of repentance. The words are true for guilty men who will humble themselves and return to their Father. However, as before, these were true words spoken to the wrong man. And Job soon said so.

4. Read 22:21 again. What command with promise is found here?

_____

This command and promise are a powerful biblical truth. While spoken to Job, who was acquainted with God, it is something we need to seriously consider in our own lives.

5. How well acquainted are you with God's character, or attributes? List ten things you know to be true about our God.

_____

_____

_____

_____

_____

_____

_____

6. How well do you think these three "comforters" were acquainted with God? What truths about God were not found in any of their countless words? Look up the following verses to find the answers.

Numbers 14:18—God is _____.

Psalm 89:1—God is _____.

Psalm 145:9—God is _____.

Jeremiah 31:3—God is _____.

Micah 7:18—God is _____.

What comfort Eliphaz, Bildad, and Zophar could have brought to Job's sore heart if they had only reminded him that God is merciful, faithful, loving, and infinitely more. With whom can you share these great truths today?

Someone has rightly said that among those professing to know Christ in our generation, scarcely one in a thousand reveals any passionate thirst for God. They are content to be shallow. They have little interest in acquainting themselves with God. "It is time for those who profess a relationship with Christ as Savior to get serious about studying the attributes of God as they are revealed in the Bible. We cannot love or trust the Lord if we do not know Him."[1]

7. In Job 22:22, what other profitable counsel did Eliphaz give Job?

How did David express this same important truth in Psalm 119:11?

Job 23, 26, and 28 are described by several authors as magnificent, and I certainly agree. Job continued in his quest to meet with the Almighty, his favorite name for God. He used it at least thirty-one times in Job, more than in any other book in the Bible.

8. What was the cry of Job's heart in 23:3-5?

In verse 6, what was he longing to receive from God?

9. Eliphaz had just told him to return to the Almighty (22:23). But what frustration did Job express in 23:3, 8-9?

David in Psalm 139:8-10 had a different cry regarding God's presence. What was it?

"Psalm 139 expresses what the believer knows; Job 23 expresses what the believer sometimes feels. Why is God sometimes so hard to find and silent when we need Him most? Or is He? This is a massive question for any suffering person."[2]

10. Although Job didn't know where God was, what did God know about him according to 23:10? What words of faith does Job express in this verse?

_____

_____

_____

_____

As we read these words in Job 23, we remember that he is in the midst of horrible suffering. Yet suddenly some of the most stirring words in the Bible fall from his lips. However rough the path we travel, Job would have us remember that God is fully aware and completely in charge of that path. This was true in Job's day and, thankfully, it is as true as ever today.

11. According to Job in 23:10 and 23:16, who was responsible for Job's trials?

_____

What words in 23:10 infer that Job knew his trials would come to an end?

_____

_____

"The time [of trial] may seem long, but I shall not be detained a moment longer than the case requires. [God] has appointed the hour of deliverance, and His time is the best time; for he is a God of knowledge, and blessed are those that wait for Him. Christians are improved and advanced by their trials, and can say, 'It is good for me that I have been afflicted (Psalm 119:71).'"[3]

12. Before the months of Job's life-changing trials, the words of God and fellowship with Him had been the greatest treasure in his life. In 23:12 how did he describe his love for God's Word?

_____

_____

13. Many men in other books of the Bible have written similar statements about the value of God's Word. What thoughts about the Word are found in the following verses?

Joshua 1:8

_____

Psalm 19:9–10

_____

Psalm 119:14

_____

Psalm 119:72

_____

Psalm 119:103

_____

Jeremiah 15:16

_____

> Holy Bible, book divine,
> Precious treasure, thou art mine;
> Mine to tell me whence I came;
> Mine to teach me what I am.
>
> ~John Burton

Over and over, Job's "miserable comforters" inferred that he was suffering because of heinous sins and wickedness in his life. In chapter 24 Job expressed his own frustration that the truly wicked and unrighteous seemingly prosper without punishment from God.

14. Read Job 24:1–11. List some of the sins that are committed by wicked men.

_____

_____

_____

To read Job's words is somewhat like reading the morning paper, isn't it?

15. What confidence in God did Job express in 24:20–24?

_____

16. While it is comforting for believers to know God's eyes are upon them, why might the words in verse 23 be very uncomfortable to proud, unbelieving people?

_____

_____

_____

After a few words of reply to Bildad in 26:1–6, Job launches into an awesome hymn of praise about the greatness and majesty of our Creator God.

17. Read Job 26:7–14. What handiwork of God is so beautifully described in these verses?

_____

_____

_____

_____

How did ancient Job know more than most modern men do about these mighty acts of God? (Hint: Read Job 23:12 again.)

_____

_____

But wait! Job had even more awesome words extolling God in chapter 28. To get there quickly, we will just glance at chapter 27. Job once again held fast to his integrity and righteousness before God (27:6) and wrote more words about wicked men reaping what they sow. Some have called these verses in chapter 27 the "hymn of the hypocrite."

We now open one of the most beautiful chapters in Job! The greatest man of Uz had once possessed many of the valuable things described in this fascinating picture of mining technology and ancient engineers at work. Once again we stand in awe of his knowledge of God's creation.

18. Read Job 28:1–19. What are some of the hidden treasures men risk their lives for while mining for underground wealth?

_____

19. Read 28:12, 20. Job wasn't interested in finding valuable treasures. What was he searching for?

_____

_____

How would you answer Job's questions? Use Scripture to support your answers. (A good place to start would be Proverbs 1:7; 2:1–10.)

_____

_____

_____

_____

20. Job answered his own question in 28:28. According to him, what is true wisdom and understanding? What does this mean?

____

____

____

"The fear of God defies our attempts at definition, because it is really another way of saying 'knowing God'. It is a heart-felt love for Him because of Who He is and what He has done; a sense of being in his majestic presence. . . . To fear God is to be sensitive to both His greatness and His graciousness. It is to know Him and to love Him whole-heartedly and unreservedly."[4]

TIMELY TRUTHS TO REMEMBER

- "It is to know Him . . ." Isn't that where we began this lesson? Eliphaz's counsel to Job was excellent advice for us all. Job himself was well acquainted with the Almighty, and certainly he was more so by the time the last chapter of this drama was written. It is my prayer that each person who studies these lessons will "acquaint now [herself] with him, and be at peace" (Job 22:21).

- Andrew Murray (1828–1917), a faithful pastor in South Africa for many years, wrote several excellent books, and many of them are still in print. *Abide in Christ* and *With Christ in the School of Prayer* have encouraged and fed believers for over one hundred years. In 1895 Mr. Murray was back in his native Scotland where he was speaker for several conferences. Missionary Amy Carmichael attended one of those meetings and was also a guest in the same home as Mr. Murray. She tells the following story of Mr. Murray's faith in His sovereign God:

  > During that stay something painful happened to Mr. Murray, and Amy records that this is how he met it.

He was quiet for a while with his Lord, then he wrote these words for himself:

First He brought me here, it is by His will I am in this place. In that fact I will rest.

Next, He will keep me here in His love, and give me grace to behave as His child. Then, He will make the trial a blessing teaching me the lessons He intends me to learn, and working in me the grace He means to bestow.

Last, in His good time He can bring me out again—how and when He knows.

As I experience this trial, Let me say I am here:

(1) By God's appointment,

(2) In His keeping,

(3) Under His training,

(4) For His time.[5]

These words are timeless, aren't they? As a matter of fact, they are similar to words spoken by Job in the last chapter of his book. I especially like his words about "grace to behave as His child." Walking in the flesh always leads us to behave in a selfish or rebellious way. How we need His power if we are to conduct ourselves as His children!

We close lesson 9 where we began, standing in awe of our great God and His wondrous works and Word. We will let the psalmist have the final word of praise:

> "Let all the earth fear the Lord: let all the
> inhabitants of the world stand in awe of him. For
> he spake and it was done." (Psalm 33:8–9)

"BE STILL, JOB!"

"Stand still, and consider the wondrous works of God." (Job 37:14)

SCRIPTURE TO READ: Job 29–37

I n an earlier lesson we mentioned that the book of Job is sometimes called the "logue book" of the Bible. In this study it is a
sign of progress that we have now rolled past two of those "logues."
Doesn't it seem like a long time since we studied the prologue? And
who is not happy we have finished all the difficult dialogues?

Before the grand epilogue in chapter 42, however, we do have thir-
teen chapters of monologues! We cover nine of those chapters in
this lesson before beginning lesson eleven and some of the grandest
chapters in the Bible. Prior to hearing from our Almighty God, we
must look at Job's last major words before he went back to scraping
his painful boils, hoping for silence at the dump. However, he didn't
get silence, for out of nowhere came a new voice with a 165-verse
monologue spoken for weary "Job's benefit!"

While the three men before him chastised Job as a sinner deserv-
ing of his troublesome situation, Elihu's purpose was more helpful.

Actually, his words helped Job take his eyes off his grievous problems, understand anew the greatness and goodness of God, and then refocus his heart to hear God's words in the final chapters of the book. Job gives no reply to Elihu, and this fourth friend receives no correction from God in the dramatic scene in chapter 42.

JOB'S MONOLOGUE — CHAPTERS 29–31

As we open the pages of these three chapters, we find what some have called "Job's autobiography." In Job 29 he remembered the good old days, followed with a look at his present painful days. Job 31 ends with yet another cry for God to hear and help him.

1. Read 29:1–6. What were some of Job's great past blessings? What were his nostalgic words in verse 2?

Perhaps we've all wished for the happy days of the past. How might dwelling on the past be a good thing? How can it sometimes be harmful? Job's past was full of walking "by [God's] light" (verse 3). Your past may be filled with many regrets of what might have been. While we can't totally forget the past, we can use it as a stepping-stone to a fruitful future.

2. What heavenly encouragements and reminders are given in Psalm 103:8–18 to help every believer?

---

3. How did Job describe his friendship and fellowship with God in 29:2–5?

_____

_____

"One feature of Job's longing for the 'good old days' is particularly striking. What Job laments first and most is the loss of God's presence and blessing."[1]

4. What testimony did Job have before men of every age and importance in Uz? See 29:7–11, 21–25.

_____

_____

Because of God's blessing on his life, how was Job able to help others (Job 29:12–17)?

_____

_____

Job had a spotless reputation of helping the poorest and neediest around him. Sadly his generosity was soon forgotten, and most of those he helped were nowhere to be found when Job's life was turned upside down. Not one of these who benefited from his kindness came to comfort him in his grief, but they did come for other reasons.

The Lord had generously given Job material wealth (Job 29). His autobiography continued as he remembered in chapter 30 that the Lord had also taken away.

5. What words in 30:1 indicate a great change in Job's life situation?

_____

_____

6. Read 30:1, 8–15. How did the same people helped by Job in happier days treat the benefactor, which commentator Matthew Henry called "the poor man's king"?

_____

Doesn't this sound somewhat like the treatment our Lord received from the ungrateful throngs He fed, healed, and taught the words of life? The cruel treatment of the "Man of Sorrows" is described in Isaiah 53: "He was wounded for our transgressions" (verse 5).

7. After reading 30:16–19, 27–30, describe Job's painful physical condition.

_____

_____

_____

_____

This description of how Job suffered is difficult to read, isn't it?

8. Job had lost all dignity, but what did he consider to be his greatest loss? See 30:20–21.

_____

Job was a great man of faith, but are you surprised to see his faith at such a low point? The last part of Job's monologue (Job 31) is clearly the words of a man of God "struggling to answer the human accusations brought against him, and to comprehend the divine sentence that seems already to have been passed . . . [it is] a moving recital of all the godly things that made up Job's life in the days before he was afflicted."[2]

We are guided through this long chapter by the little word _if_, used at least fifteen times to inform us of sins that were not a part of Job's life. Some think he was reminding God, and others around the ash pile, of his righteousness. For certain he was defending himself for the last time against all the harsh charges thrown around by the three nonwise men. Surely three frowning faces were looking at him as he spoke.

9. Read Job 31:1–32 to answer these questions:

What moral sins had Job turned away from (verses 1, 9–12)?

_____

How had he treated his employees (verses 13–15)?

_____

How had he shared his wealth with others (verses 16–28)?

_____

How had he shown kindness and hospitality (verses 29–32)?

_____

You may find other examples, but these will give you an overall picture of actions Job did, or did not do, because he desired to be a righteous man who feared God.

10. In 31:35–37, what was Job still longing for?

_____

_____

11. Do you think Job 31 exhibits self-righteousness on Job's part? Do you think he was saying, "I have lived right before God, and still He punishes me without cause or explanation"? Was Job inferring that God is not fair? Explain.

_____

_____

_____

_____

Layton Talbert writes,

> It is tempting to interpret [Job 31] as a prime example of self-righteousness, but to do so would fly in the face of Job's just call for vindication. Indeed, it would undermine the book's depiction of Job as a genuinely righteous and blameless man. [We must remember] that God never directly rebukes Job for pride. Nor does He correct Job for self-righteousness, per se.[3]

ELIHU'S MONOLOGUE

Respected Bible commentators either like Elihu or dislike him as much as they did the other three friends. He broke the silence at the dump just when we think the word war was over. Was he just another blowhard with nothing new to say? I'll admit this was exactly my thinking. But having read his many words over and over, I've now come to appreciate this young man who was a true friend to Job. His response to Job's suffering was, for the most part, kind and sympathetic. He had a high opinion of our God, and he helped Job refocus his eyes toward heaven in preparation for the only monologue that really counted—God's.

Elihu was a young man with plenty of words stored up for Job and the three windy comforters. We will take a very brief look at chapters 32–35. The rest of this lesson will be spent primarily in chapters 36–37.

12. Read Job 32:2–15. Why was Elihu angry at Job?

Why was he angry at the three friends?

What was the response of the three to Elihu?

---

13. Read 32:8; 33:4; 34:10; 34:12; and 35:13. What name for God did Elihu use in these verses?

_____

As mentioned in an earlier lesson, this is Job's favorite name for God, and apparently Elihu's favorite also.

14. What does it mean when we speak of our God as the Almighty One? (Consult a Bible dictionary if necessary.)

_____

_____

El Shaddai means, "the One mighty to nourish, satisfy, and supply."[4] He is the One strong enough to help us in every situation, the giver of strength, and the satisfier of His people. He is our all-sufficient One, Whose grace is sufficient for all our days.

Notice how many truths about the Almighty are included in J. Paul Williams's tribute to our Almighty Father. Underline these truths as you meditate on his words.

> Almighty Father, You alone are holy,
> You are my refuge, I will trust in You.
> You are a tower, a mighty fortress,
> You are my strength and shield,
> You are God.
>
> Almighty Father, You alone are holy,
> You are Creator, You are all in all!
> Yours is the power, Yours is the glory,
> Yours is the majesty,
> You are God.[5]

15. What promises did Elihu make to Job in 33:7 and 33:32–33?

_____

_____

Of what did he accuse Job in 33:13?

_____

16. How did Elihu describe Job's physical affliction in 33:19–22?

_____

_____

_____

_____

_____

_____

Amy Carmichael described people like those who visited Job as "the unwounded who had never suffered." She wondered how they, who had never had as much as one boil on their body, could understand the anguish of a man covered with boils? In her twenty years of suffering, she learned to thank God even for visitors who sometimes "trampled unawares upon [her], talking sweet nothings."[6] May we who enjoy good health remember her words when visiting friends whose days and sleepless nights know only continual suffering.

17. In Job 34–37 Elihu described many truths about God's character. Read the following verses and list what he said about our God:

Job 34:10, 12—God is _____

Job 34:21—God is _____

Job 36:4—God is _____

Job 36:26—God is _____

Job 37:5–13—God is _____

Job 37:14—God is _____

Job 37:23—God is _____

18. Elihu, a keen observer of creation, described specific works of our Almighty Creator in 36:27–37:22. After reading these verses, find the following acts of our God:

The rain cycle is described in verses _____.

Thunderstorms are described in verses _____.

God's rule over snow and ice is described in verses _____.

His rule over the clouds is described in verses _____.

His rule over animals is described in verses _____.

His rule over all weather is described in verses _____.

Always remember, it is the "Ruler of all Nature" Who sends our weather, not Mother Nature! He sends what is best for every area of the earth. No matter what present-day environmentalists say, His weather is always right, for He is always righteous.

19. In light of these great descriptions of our "Ruler of all Nature," what was Elihu's command to Job in 37:14?

_____

_____

These powerful words helped prepare Job for the soon-to-come meeting with God. This is good counsel, is it not? How we need to stand still and always remember the countless wondrous works God continually brings before our eyes. All His creation continually sings about the mighty power of our God and displays His wonderful handiwork for all men to plainly see (Psalm 19:1–4).

✺✺✺✺✺ TIMELY TRUTHS TO REMEMBER ✺✺✺✺✺

✒ Read Job 36:26 once again. Elihu's declaration, "We know him not," could be the life verse for too many believers in our Bible-preaching churches. How well can your tongue describe His character?

Job 37:14 is the theme verse for this lesson: "Stand still, and consider the wondrous works of God." Moses used a similar command in Exodus 14:13: "Stand still, and see the salvation of the Lord." David wrote an almost identical truth in Psalm 46:10: "Be still, and know that I am God."

What does the Bible mean when it commands us to "stand still" or "be still"? Isn't it telling us to be quiet, take our hands off our situation, and wait patiently for Him? It is also a command to trust God to do what is right, even when we don't understand and to be content with changes He chooses for us. I believe the German hymn writer Katharina von Schlegel (1697–1768) understood the meaning of "Be Still." Read prayerfully the words of her lovely hymn, and then ask Almighty God to help you bear patiently any cross or grief He places into your life.

Be still, my soul: the Lord is on thy side;
Bear patiently the cross of grief or pain;
Leave to thy God to order and provide;
In ev'ry change He faithful will remain.
Be still, my soul: thy best, thy heav'nly Friend
Through thorny ways leads to a joyful end.

Be still, my soul: thy God doth undertake
To guide the future as He has the past.
Thy hope, thy confidence let nothing shake;
All now mysterious shall be bright at last.
Be still my soul: the waves and winds still know
His voice Who ruled them while He dwelt below.

~Katharina von Schlegel

"HOW GREAT THOU ART"

"O Lord my God, thou art very great; thou art
clothed with honour and majesty." (Psalm 104:1)

<small>SCRIPTURE TO READ:</small> Job 38–41

In the chapters so far we have been eager, along with suffering Job, to hear God's voice. In this lesson His majestic voice is clearly heard by all at the Uz town dump. What will be His first words to suffering Job? Will He pour soothing oil into his wounds and explain the reason for his many tortured days and nights? Will He tell him his long ordeal is soon to be over?

God could have said these things, but He didn't. When He broke His silence, He didn't give Job any answers to his numerous questions. Neither did He apologize for His long silence. He didn't mention His earlier meetings with the wicked one and the limited permissions He allowed Satan to have over Job's life.

Actually, what God did say in chapters 38–41 is a surprise. Why did a man on an ash pile need to hear about the foundation of the earth, the sun, the moon, the seas, the rain cycle, lightning, wild goats, an ugly ostrich, a hippopotamus, and a fierce alligator?

"This mountain range of a monologue by the Lord overshadows all that has been said. God started this whole affair, and God will finish it. The monologue reminds us that the book of Job is not ultimately about Job or suffering after all; it is about God and our relationship to Him."[1]

Of all the lessons in this series, I feel more inadequate to write this one than all the others. The magnificence of our wonderful God in these chapters is truly awe inspiring. Who is so great as our God? Who but the Almighty could take us on a tour of His universe, and then treat us to a marvelous parade of His creatures? As we read these Scriptures, we are reminded again that He reigns wondrously over all His creation, and that includes every detail of our lives. "Praise to the Lord, the Almighty, the King of Creation!"

"THY POWER THROUGHOUT THE UNIVERSE DISPLAYED"—JOB 38:1–38

1. The Lord did not answer Job in a still, small voice. Read 38:1. What was the setting for His words to Job?

___

What were God's first words to Job (38:2–3) and what did He mean?

___

___

___

___

God now had a seventy-seven-question science exam for Job. Job would, no doubt, find himself shrinking in importance as these amazing questions were asked. Somehow his runny sores, and his ash pile, shrank in importance when God was present at the dump.

2. Read Job 38:4–6. What question did God ask Job regarding the creation of the earth?

_____

_____

Who sang and shouted their joyful approval of God's mighty work (38:7)?

_____

3. According to Job 38:8–11, 16, what power does God have over the sea?

_____

How does He restrain its mighty force?

_____

Job got a refresher course on the greatness and power of our sovereign God. We marvel at the entire monologue. Its beauty causes us once again to stand in awe of our wonderful God! Only the Ancient of Days could answer these questions. Puny man has tried to understand and answer them for centuries, all the while denying the great God Who put all this into motion.

4. God continued with more humbling questions for Job in 38:12–38. What were the many powers and wonders of creation described here so beautifully?

_____

_____

_____

_____

I sing the mighty power of God,
That made the mountains rise;
That spread the flowing seas abroad,
And built the lofty skies.
I sing the wisdom that ordained
The sun to rule the day;
The moon shines full at His command,
And all the stars obey.

~Isaac Watts

"ALL CREATURES GREAT AND SMALL"—JOB 38:39–41

The Almighty followed with a few zoology questions for Job, who didn't do any better on this part of the exam than he had done with the earlier questions relating to physical science. What a parade of animals we have in this portion of Scripture! Notice the minute details God gives for these varied creatures. Some are feared by man, others are afraid of man, but all are like household pets to God. He created them, He sustains each one, and He alone takes their breath away. Like us, they all borrow life from Him. What a testimony to His greatness and goodness!

5. Read Job 38:39–39:8. What untamed creatures did God question Job about in these verses?

_____

How did God oversee their care?

_____

6. What unusual creatures did the "King of Creation" speak of in Job 39:9–18?

_____

How did these animals depend on God for their care?

_____

"Thou openest thine hand and satisfiest the
desire of every living thing." (Psalm 145:16)

7. Why does the ostrich especially need God's care (Job 39:13–18)?

_____

_____

Most animals nourish their young, but how does this silly animal treat hers? Some human parents are sometimes like the ostrich in the care of their children, just as silly and careless. Their hearts are hardened against God, preferring to enjoy their sins, even if it means neglecting or destroying their little ones. Isn't verse 16 a description of many who frequent present-day abortion centers? The ostrich will not stand accountable for her actions, but certainly those who treat God's little children as nothing but inconveniences in their life will know His wrath at the judgment (Matthew 18:6).

8. How is the war horse beautifully described in Job 39:19–25?

_____

How have these horses played a part in the history of all nations?

_____

The horsepower we use today is much different from what is described here, isn't it? God made this mighty creature to serve his earthly master and do his bidding. He is useful only as he willingly submits to his rider. This is a great truth for us to ponder because our usefulness to our Master also demands complete surrender.

9. Read Job 39:26–30. What two birds are mentioned here as examples of God's wisdom and power?

_____

He gave us eyes to see them,
And lips that we might tell
How great is God Almighty,
Who has made all things well.

~Mrs. C. F. Alexander

God asked Job many questions, and from his ash pile Job offered nothing. A very quiet and subdued Job wrapped his rags more closely around him and gave his full attention to God. Undoubtedly he realized just how many things he did not know. But God was not finished, and in Job 40 the Almighty had a miniature dialogue with Job. It ended with some signs of much-needed humbling on Job's part.

10. Job 40:2 mentions man contending with God. What is the sin behind such arguing? Read Proverbs 13:10 to find your answer.

_____

When we have a proud heart, do we have a high opinion of ourselves or a high opinion of God?

_____

11. How did Job describe himself in Job 40:4?

_____

12. What does Job's brief answer to God in 40:3–5 say about his heart condition? Was his attitude one like that found in 1 Peter 5:6 or the one found in Proverbs 16:18?

_____

_____

Earlier God had testified to Job's holiness, and in several of Job's dialogues his words showed his faith to be strong. (We must not forget his statement in Job 13:15: "Though he slay me, yet will I trust in him.") As his weariness stretched into many months, God's silence did not cause Job to cast away his confidence in God.

13. When we're not trusting God, who are we trusting? What is the warning in Proverbs 3:5?

_____

_____

Instead of casting away our confidence, what should be our response? First Peter 5:7 says, "Casting all your care upon him, for he careth for you." If we obey this command, Psalm 55:22 promises, "Cast thy burden upon the Lord, and he shall sustain thee: he shall never suffer the righteous to be moved."

14. What question did God ask Job in 40:9?

_____

A hymn we often sing states, "The arm of flesh will fail you, you dare not trust your own." How weak are our arms, but how strong are the arms of God!

15. Read the following verses and write down what He has declared about His arms:

Exodus 15:16

_____

Psalm 77:15

_____

Psalm 89:13

_____

Psalm 98:1

_____

16. How is God's arm also described in Deuteronomy 33:27?

_____

> "Faint not nor fear, His arms are near,
> He changeth not, and thou art dear;
> Only believe and thou shalt see,
> That Christ is all in all to thee."[2]

Our arms are not strong enough to hold us up in times of grief and suffering, and neither were Job's. God invites us, as His children, to rest in His strong, everlasting arms. What have we to dread, what have we to fear, when we are leaning on His everlasting arms? Job ran, as one author describes it, from out of his storm into God's mighty arms.

God, however, thought Job needed more teaching and humbling. To accomplish this purpose, He brought to Job's attention two monstrous and mighty animals who are examples of those who submit to God and trust Him for their every need.

17. Read Job 40:15–24. Read carefully the description of this mighty land animal, behemoth. What did he eat (verses 15, 20)?

_____

Describe his strength (verses 16, 18).

_____

Where did he live (verses 21–22)?

_____

How thirsty was he (verse 23)?

_____

As mighty as he was, Who controlled him (verse 19)?

_____

Does this sound like any animal you've ever seen in a zoo? If you're thinking of a hippopotamus, a rhinoceros, or even a brontosaurus, you're probably close. The important thing is, God created him and has sustained him for centuries. Never has this king of the jungle quarreled with his Creator or questioned His ability to care for all his needs. Nor has the great sea creature God now describes.

18. Read Job 41:1–34. How has puny man attempted to contain, or control, this mighty creature called leviathan? Has he succeeded in these attempts?

Such a creature may overwhelm man, but the king of the sea is no match for the King of Creation. Job 41:11 says, "Whatsoever is under the whole heaven is mine."

God places this principle of ownership in the middle of His discussion about a monstrous sea creature, and He does so not just for Job's benefit but for ours also. He created, or made possible, everything we have. Because He owns it, He can, without explanation to us, take back anything we have. Layton Talbert says: "Do we grasp [this truth] in our souls and live it? That is what affliction tests."[3]

19. Read Psalm 104:25–29. How are God's wondrous sea creatures, including leviathan, described by the psalmist?

The psalmist sprinkles plenty of praise throughout his great words about God and His creation. He cannot think of God's handiwork without rejoicing. It is my prayer that this lesson will somehow do the same for you. Meditating on these powerful chapters in Job, along with the majesty of Psalm 104, should cause our hearts to cry out: "O Lord my God, thou art very great; thou art clothed with honour and majesty" (Psalm 104:1).

✠✠✠ TIMELY TRUTHS TO REMEMBER ✠✠✠

✠ Along with Job, God has in these chapters taken us on a walking tour of His great and mighty creation. From Job's words in chapter 40 we sense his feeling of insignificance. Do not our hearts feel the same? David, the writer of Psalm 8:4, expressed similar amazement when he said, "What is man, that thou art mindful of him?"

✠ Why should sinful, weak, miserable man, who is continually forgetful of his Creator, deserve any attention from the Lord of glory? But He surrounds us with such attention because He loves us with an everlasting love (Jeremiah 31:3) and has reconciled us unto Himself through our Lord Jesus Christ (2 Corinthians 5:18).

✠ In Philippians 3:10, the apostle Paul cried out, "That I may know him!" Paul was, at this time, an old man and had been walking with God for many years. His cry reminds us that we are never to be satisfied with our knowledge of God. There is always something new to discover, or rediscover. After the awesome chapters we have studied in this lesson, we are reminded not just of God's power and wonder alone. We are reminded that this same God is our heavenly Father and that we are "worth more to him than many sparrows" (Matthew 10:31). We are also worth far more to Him than even the great and mighty creatures found in His monologue to Job.

O Lord my God! When I in awesome wonder
Consider all the worlds Thy hands have made;
I see the stars, I hear the rolling thunder,
Thy pow'r throughout the universe displayed.

And when I think that God, His Son not sparing,
Sent Him to die—I scarce can take it in:
That on the Cross, my burden gladly bearing,
He bled and died to take away my sin.

Then sings my soul, my Savior God, to Thee,
HOW GREAT THOU ART! HOW GREAT THOU ART!
Then sings my soul, my Savior God, to Thee,
HOW GREAT THOU ART! HOW GREAT THOU ART!

~Stuart K. Hine

> "All thy works shall praise thee, O Lord; and thy saints
> shall bless thee. They shall speak of the glory of thy
> kingdom, and talk of thy power." (Psalm 145:10–11)

JOB'S HAPPY ENDING

"For he maketh sore, and bindeth up; he woundeth,
and his hands make whole." (Job 5:18)

SCRIPTURE TO READ: Job 42

Centuries after Job lived, the apostle James commanded believers to remember great Bible men who were "example[s] of suffering affliction, and of patience" (James 5:10). The writer then gave us the name of one such man: Job.

Reminding his Jewish readers of God's persevering man in Uz, James went on in 5:11 to write, "Ye have heard of the patience of Job, and have seen the end of the Lord." (The last phrase of the verse means the results of the Lord's dealings with Job.) In this last lesson we will see how Job's story ended, and then with Job, we will dust off our ashes and join a large crowd of friends and family at the home of Job and his wife.

Prior to leaving the dump, however, we must take careful notice of Job's submissive attitude in the early verses of Job 42. This touching scene is followed by God's humbling of Job's three miserable comforters. Would our humbled Job be willing to forgive and pray for these who added to his affliction by continually claiming he was a wicked man with secret sins?

Before opening the epilogue to Job's story, let's briefly return to the book of James. In referring to James 5:11 earlier, I purposely failed to comment on the last nine words of the verse. Here James reminds us that the reason for the happy ending to Job's life was that "the Lord is very pitiful, and of tender mercy." Our compassionate and merciful God is seen in the last chapter of Job binding up Job's wounds and healing his broken heart.

Job was not the hero of the book that bears his name. No, reader, it is our loving, faithful, and Almighty God, Whose character is the main theme of Job. We learn much about suffering from Job, but we learn more about the greatness of God to sustain all His children when they suffer afflictions allowed in their lives by their sovereign Lord.

While we are perhaps not like Job physically, spiritually, or materially, our God is exactly the same as Job's. He is still Almighty, and He knows our ways as well as He knew Job's. He has not changed, nor will He ever. With James we give praise that He is still "very pitiful, and of tender mercy" (James 5:11).

JOB'S REPENTANCE—JOB 42:1-6.

1. What statement of unrestrained admiration did Job declare about God in Job 42:2?

_____

_____

This is not just a statement of God's boundless power, but it relays a deeper meaning as a statement on the sovereignty of God. The verse could be read, "God can do anything He chooses and nothing can hinder or overrule His purposes and plans."

2. What were Job's words of repentance in 42:3?

_____

3. What sins might Job have been repenting of? A look at the following verses from earlier chapters in Job will help you with your answers.

3:3, 11–12

_____

6:8–9

_____

7:15–16

_____

9:17

_____

13:24–25

_____

23:16

_____

30:20–21

_____

"[Job] tacitly confesses that he may have said in his bitterness many an unwise and unseemly thing. Therefore, he bows his head before the Lord his God and confesses that he has darkened counsel by words without knowledge and uttered things he understood not. Notwithstanding, the man of God proceeds to draw near unto the Lord, before whom he bows himself."[1]

4. When he wrote James 4:6–10, perhaps the apostle was thinking of Job's humility before God in Job 42. What comfort, and challenge, did James give for all who, like Job, desire to draw nearer to God?

_____

_____

_____

_____

We are never nearer God than when we are low and bow at His feet in humility. May our cry always be "Nearer, still nearer." Read James 4:10 again. When we humble ourselves before Him, what does He promise us?

_____

5. Read Job 42:4–5. One author states that verse 5 "is the climax of the book and the objectives of God's own speeches."[2] Do you agree with his statement? Explain your answer.

_____

_____

6. Having a clearer view of our holy God will lead us to lower thoughts of ourselves. How did Job express this in 42:6?

_____

_____

"The more you appreciate God, the more you will depreciate yourself. While the thought of God rises higher and higher, you also will sink lower and lower in your own esteem. The word used by Job, 'I abhor myself,' is a strong one. It might be paraphrased thus, 'I nauseate myself. I am disgusted with myself.' When we adore God, we shall abhor self."[3]

7. If Job's story had ended with verse 6, would Job have been a happy, contented man? Even if it meant suffering alone at the dump forever? Explain your answer.

_____

_____

_____

_____

The last glimpse of happiness in this great book was found in chapter 1. We are grateful for this final chapter where we see righteous Job still at the dump, still covered with boils, but now surrounded by God's peace. After hearing God's words, and humbly bowing before Him, he was at peace. He then made his ash pile an altar where he gladly worshiped. New joy now filled his soul, but before this joy was fully celebrated, he must learn of God's dealings with his three friends.

GOD'S REBUKE AND RESTORATION—JOB 42:7-10

8. Read Job 42:7. Why did God chastise Eliphaz, Bildad, and Zophar?

_____

9. What were some of the wrong things they had spoken about God, and Job? A review of the following verses will help you with your answer.

8:6

_____

11:3

_____

15:5

_____

20:5

_____

20:19

_____

22:5–10

_____

22:23

_____

10. Why did God not include Elihu in this chastisement? Review Elihu's monologue in lesson 10 to help with your answer.

_____

11. According to 42:8, what were the three friends commanded to do in order to be reconciled to God? What part was Job to have in their reconciliation?

_____

_____

How was Job's forgiveness of the three a testimony to the genuineness of his words and actions in verses 2–6?

_____

_____

12. If the three friends had chosen not to obey God's instructions, what would He have done to them (42:8)?

_____

_____

13. God restored Job's losses when Job showed forgiveness through what act of humility in 42:10?

_____

"There is no better therapy for a wounded or bitter spirit toward those who have wronged you than praying for them. God expects no less from us than He did from Job. Pray for those who have wronged you particularly in the context of your suffering. It is the mark of humility, maturity, and Christlikeness."[4]

The last statement of 42:10 is "the Lord gave Job twice as much as he had before." How did the amazing news spread about the mighty storm at the dump, the sound of God's voice, Job and three of his friends on their faces, and the sacrificing of bulls and rams as a sacrifice for sin? We hope Job's wife was one of the first to hear. We don't know how she spent her months of unspeakable sorrow, but this next portion of Job reveals that the husband she had once counseled to curse God and die was home again. At first he was probably still in his rags, but the joy on his face certainly brought long-awaited hope to her heart!

JOB'S RECEPTION AND REWARD, JOB 42:11–17

According to 42:11, Job's brothers, sisters, and acquaintances dropped by to visit Job after his return from the dump. Although they had forsaken him when he was on the ash pile, they came to comfort him and bring him gifts.

14. Job 42:12 describes God's material blessings upon His servant. What were these?

_____

_____

We are not told when Job's wife fell humbly before her Creator. When did she repent for her foolish counsel to her husband in Job 2:9? God didn't reveal this to us, but had she continued to

curse God, her hard heart would have robbed her of the blessings described in 42:11–15. Repentance and forgiveness are one
important theme in this last chapter. But perhaps the greatest
truth here is the long-suffering, mercy, love, and faithfulness of
Almighty God.

15. Read 42:13–15. According to these verses, how did God show His
goodness to Job and his wife?

_____

"Long-time missionary in the hills of Kentucky, Mrs. L. C. East-
erling, once confided her homespun observation on the preser-
vation of Job's wife. When God finally blessed Job with a new
family, she remarked, guess who had to have ten more children
all over again?"[5]

16. Since God gave Job twice as many animals as before, why do you
think He did not give him twice as many children?

_____

What blessings this couple would have missed if Job had followed
his wife's foolish counsel earlier in the book! How they must have
enjoyed their three lovely daughters and seven sons. "The blessing of
the Lord, it maketh rich" (Proverbs 10:22).

In lesson 3, I shared with you a poem about Job's wife's faithless response to her loss and grief. In the light of the events of chapter 42, I
now share the last two verses of Esther Archibald's insightful words:

> "Trust God and live through good and ill,"
> Job taught this fretful wife.
> He passed the test.
> She, too, was blessed
> Through his victorious life.

> God gave to them ten children more,
> Job's health and wealth restored.
> His patient life
> Convinced his wife
> 'Twas best to trust the Lord.
>
> ~Esther Archibald[6]

17. Healed and restored to a greater walk with God, how many additional years did God's servant, Job, live (42:16)?

_____

From his ten children were many descendants. When they met for future family reunions in Uz, how many generations were present around the tables?

_____

❋❋❋ TIMELY TRUTHS TO REMEMBER ❋❋❋

🦋 "Job's greatest blessing was not the regaining of his health and wealth or the rebuilding of his family and circle of friends. His greatest blessing was knowing God better and understanding His workings in a deeper way."[7] Through this study of Job, have you come to a greater love for God? What truths about God have you seen on display in Job? Have you submitted yourself, and the events of your life, to the hands of our sovereign and righteous God?

🦋 Job's months of suffering had a happy ending, but God never revealed His reasons for Job's loss and misery. In the wisdom of God, not all endings give cause for rejoicing. Perhaps our health remains the same or even worsens, someone we love dearly dies after suffering, or a rebellious child continues in his rebellion against God and those who love him. Like Job, we may never know the reason God chooses to deal with us as He does. However, a knowledge of our Father's character will eventually help us to agree with these words of the psalmist: "He is righteous in all his ways, and holy in all his works" (Psalm 145:17). Perhaps the unknown author of the following poem experienced great sorrow that he never understood this side of heaven. From his experience came these words to encourage us:

Not now, but in the coming years.
It may be in the better land
We'll read the meaning of our tears,
And there, some time we'll understand.
God knows the way, He holds the key,
He guides us with unerring hand;
Some time with tearless eye we'll see;
Yes there, up there, we'll understand.[8]

A faithful servant of God, Dr. Lehman Strauss (1911–97), had his faith in our sovereign God severely tested due to a debilitating stroke that left his wife of fifty-one years a helpless invalid until her death. As he lived through this trial of his faith, Dr. Strauss read and profited greatly from the book of Job. In testimony as to how this great book helped him, he wrote:

> I expect to meet Job one day. I will thank him for his rich legacy. He has helped me to regard my trial, not as the fiery darts of Satan (Ephesians 6:16), but as "the arrows of the Almighty" (Job 6:4). He who sent the arrows has bound up and dressed the wounds. In His own time and for His good purpose, He will heal them perfectly. "Though he slay me, yet will I trust in him" (Job 13:15).[9]

It is difficult to know how to end these lessons on this amazing book. I could remind you again of the themes we've mentioned often: our response to our suffering and our response to others who are suffering. While having biblical responses is key to our walk with God and victory in trials, there is something more important. How we respond is, in the long run, determined by our knowledge of God's character. Although Job was a perfect and upright man who feared God and hated evil (1:1), he still needed to have a greater knowledge of his God. So do we. It matters not how long we've been saved and serving our Lord. May we give ourselves to know not just of God but His character as He has revealed it in Scripture.

Job did little singing at the dump (Job 30:31). But I believe his repentance and restoration to fellowship with God brought a new song to his heart, and surely his song was not about how hard life was on the ash pile! No, I believe his new song was about the marvelous God, Who had shown mercy and long-suffering to him. It was also a song of praise for new opportunities to serve God. Imagine having 140 more years to live and serve! With his large family gathered around him, maybe he would take out his once-silenced harp and sing a song of praise.

ENDNOTES

LESSON ONE

1. Peter Williams, *From Despair to Hope* (Surrey, England: Day One Publications, 2002), 11.

2. C. H. Spurgeon, Sermon 352, Metropolitan Tabernacle Pulpit, www.spurgeongems.org.

3. Warren W. Wiersbe, *Be Patient* (Wheaton, IL: Victor Books, 1991), 16.

4. Williams, 16.

LESSON TWO

1. Williams, 20.

2. Alexander Whyte, *Bible Characters from the Old Testament and the New Testament* (Grand Rapids, MI: Zondervan, 1967), 379.

3. Jim Berg, *When Trouble Comes* (Greenville, SC: BJU Press, 2002), 12.

4. *Biblical Viewpoint: Focus on Job* (Greenville, SC: Bob Jones University, 1987), 5–6.

LESSON THREE

1. Gian Karssen, *Her Name Is Woman* (Colorado Springs: NavPress, 1975), 124.

2. Layton Talbert, *Beyond Suffering* (Greenville, SC: BJU Press, 2007), 65.

3. John Phillips, *Exploring the Scriptures* (Chicago: Moody Bible Institute, 1965), 101.

4. George Sweeting, *Who Said That?* (Chicago: Moody Press, 1994), 114.

5. Esther Archibald, *Sourcebook of Poetry*, compiled by Al Bryant (Grand Rapids, MI: Zondervan, 1992), 631.

6. Talbert, 7.

LESSON FOUR

1. Amy Carmichael, *Rose from Brier* (Fort Washington, PA: Christian Literature Crusade, 1973), 152.

2. Derek Thomas, *Mining for Wisdom* (Darlington, England: Evangelical Press, 2002), 46.

3. J. Vernon McGee, *Thru the Bible with J. Vernon McGee*, vol. 2 (Pasadena, CA: Thru the Bible Radio, 1982), 592–93.

4. Talbert, 85.

5. Wiersbe. 22–23.

6. Jill Briscoe, *Out of the Storm and into God's Arms* (Colorado Springs: Waterbrook Press, 2000), 58.

7. Ron Hamilton, "How Can I Fear," *Majesty Hymns* (Greenville, SC: Majesty Music, 1997), 412.

LESSON FIVE

1. Talbert, 5–6.

2. A. B. Simpson, quoted in *Streams in the Desert*, Mrs. Charles E. Cowman (Ulrichsville, OH: Barbour Publishing, n.d.).

3. Dennis R. Petersen, *Unlocking the Mysteries of Creation* (El Dorado, CA: Creation Resource Publications, 2002), 194–95.

4. Carmichael, 150.

5. Samuel Rideout, *The Book of Job* (Neptune, NJ: Loizeaux Brothers, Inc, 1976), 32.

LESSON SIX

1. Charles H. Spurgeon, *The Salt-Cellars*, vol. II (Pasadena, TX: Pilgrim Publications, 1975), 11.

2. Carmichael, 28.

LESSON SEVEN

1. Mike Mason, *The Gospel According to Job* (Wheaton, IL: Crossway, 1994), 213.

2. Talbert, 4, 18.

3. Charles H. Spurgeon, *Morning and Evening* (Grand Rapids, MI: Zondervan, 1971), 450.

4. Joseph Caryl, quoted by Horatius Bonar, *Words Old and New* (Edinburgh: Banner of Truth Trust, 1994), 171.

5. Lucy A. Bennett, quoted by Elisabeth Elliot, *The Music of His Promises* (Ann Arbor, MI: Servant Publications, 2000), 171.

6. Charles H. Spurgeon, quoted by Arthur W. Pink, *The Attributes of God* (Grand Rapids, MI: Baker Book House, 1975), 32.

7. Ella Wheeler Wilcox, quoted by Bryant, 293.

LESSON EIGHT

1. H. H. Rowley, *Job* (London: Oliphants, Marshall, Morgan and Scott, 1976), 116.

2. *Biblical Viewpoint*, 24–25.

3. Carmichael, 144, 164.

4. Barry Lyall and Lew King, "The Keeper of Your Soul" (Dayton, OH: Lorenz Publishing Company, 2003).

LESSON NINE

1. Randy Jaeggli, *More like the Master* (Greenville, SC: Ambassador International, 2004), 6–7.

2. Talbert, 133.

3. Rev. William Jay, *Evening Exercises* (Harrisonburg, VA: Sprinkle Publications, 1999), 706.

4. Thomas, 127–28.

5. V. Raymond Edman, *They Found the Secret* (Grand Rapids, MI: Zondervan Publishing House, 1960), 117–18.

LESSON TEN

1. Talbert, 154.

2. Talbert, 158.

3. Talbert, 159.

4. Nathan Stone, *Names of God* (Chicago: Moody Press, 1944), 34.

5. J. Paul Williams, "Almighty Father" (Delaware Water Gap, PA: Shawnee Press, Inc., 1994).

6. Amy Carmichael, adapted, 20.

LESSON ELEVEN

1. Talbert, 197.

2. Charles H. Spurgeon, *Morning and Evening*, 407.

3. Talbert, 214.

LESSON TWELVE

1. Charles H. Spurgeon, Sermon 2009, 1.

2. *Biblical Viewpoint*, 41.

3. Charles H. Spurgeon, Sermon 2009, 5.

4. Talbert, 234.

5. Talbert, 303.

6. Bryant, 631.

7. Wiersbe, 155.

8. *Biblical Viewpoint*, 48.

9. Lehman Strauss, *In God's Waiting Room* (Chicago: Moody Press, 1984), 38.